Arger

The
Business Traveller's
Handbook

Argentina
The Business Traveller's Handbook

published by
Gorilla Guides
128 Kensington Church Street
London W8 4BH
Tel: 44 20 7221 7166   Fax: 44 20 7792 9288
E-mail: stacey.international@virgin.net

ISBN: 1 903185 0 41

CIP Data: A catalogue record for this book is available from the British Library

© Gorilla Guides 2000

Series Editor: Max Scott
Production: Kitty Carruthers & Sam Crooks
Design: Nimbus Design
Printing & Binding: Tien Wah Press Ltd

The author and publisher have made every effort to ensure that the facts in this handbook are accurate and up-to-date. The reader is recommended, however, to verify travel and visa arrangements with a suitable consular office or airline agent before departure. The author and publisher cannot accept any responsibility for loss, injury or inconvenience, however caused.

None of the maps in this book are designed to have any political significance.

Picture credits: Pages 7(br) & 8 Bob Green. All other photographs courtesy of Ffotograff. *Half title (tl & tr)* Sandra Doble; *(bl)* John Harrison, *(br)* Stuart Turpin. *pp.5 & 7 (tr)* Sandra Doble; *p.6(t)* Fabienne Fossez; *p.6 (b)* Stuart Turpin.

This page: A memorial to the volunteer firefighters of La Boca stands out against the town's typically colourful house fronts *(Sandra Doble)*.

Argentina

The Business Traveller's Handbook

Bob Green

Oblivious to their surroundings, a solitary couple dance in Buenos Aires' Plaza Diablo.

▼ The statue of General San Martín proudly overlooks the Plaza de Mayo in Buenos Aires.

▲ The grave of Eva Perón in the Recoleta district of Buenos Aires is still constantly tended by her admirers.

▲ The spectacular Iguazú Falls, on the border between Brazil and Argentina; two million litres of water pass over the Falls every second.

◀ The imposing neo-Classical entrance to Buenos Aires' Metropolitan Cathedral.

▶ The Argentine flag flutters over the Malvinas War Memorial in Buenos Aires.

Acknowledgements

Thanks to my friends in Buenos Aires, Elida Messina and Jorge and Beba Meinardo, for their friendship over the decades and their great gift of welcoming a stranger into their family lives. For me, no visit to Buenos Aires would be complete without them!

Casa Rosada – the Government Seat – in the capital's Plaza de Mayo is the political and administrative centre of the Republic.

CONTENTS

Argentina yesterday and today

1

Argentina yesterday and today

Argentina is the second largest country in South America. It covers nearly 2,800,000 sq.km.,which makes it about as big as all of western Europe and the eighth biggest country in the world - only slightly smaller than India. The land surface is equivalent to about 30 per cent of the United States of America and is almost the total land area south of the Tropic of Capricorn east of the Andes apart from Uruguay and some small areas of Brazil and Paraguay. If you set out to walk the length of Argentina from the frontier with Bolivia to the frozen wastes of Tierra del Fuego at Cape Horn you would cover 3,500 km. – the equivalent of walking from Spain to Finland or from Alaska to Florida. The first thing a visitor must try and come to terms with is the sheer size of this vast and complex country.

Geography

In the north, the sprawling forests and grasslands of the Gran Chaco, which run through Bolivia and Paraguay, spill over into Argentina. The west is marked by the permanently snow-capped peaks of the mighty Andes, second in height only to the Himalayas and the longest mountain range on earth. They stretch over 7,000 km. down the Pacific length of South America. On the north-eastern frontier, Argentina shares a humid and semi-tropical border with Paraguay and Brazil, as well as the more temperate lands of Uruguay. To the west and south of Buenos Aires the grassy plains of central Argentina, the Pampas, cover 650,000 sq.km. Below the Pampas to the south the plains give way to the bleak and windswept plateau of Patagonia, an immense area of 770,000 sq.km. This dry and freezing land with little vegetation is sparsely inhabited even today.

1

Before the Europeans Arrived
Unlike the mighty empires of the Aztecs in Mexico and the Incas of Peru, the indigenous peoples of what is now Argentina were not united under any strong central social or military government.

Although some small archaeological sites dating from 9000 BC have been discovered, there are few relics of the past, apart from cave paintings in Los Toldos and stone stelae in Tucumán province. The population east of the Andes was small and widely scattered. Hunting and gathering and, along the coast, fishing, were still the most important activities.

> **Argentines**
>
> The Republic is home to almost 37 million Argentines, the vast majority of whom are Spanish speaking. The average Argentine citizen can expect to live well into his seventies. Fewer than 4 per cent live outside a city or town, and there is a much lower crime rate than most American or European cities. Argentina (especially Buenos Aires) has become one of the world's most developed societies outside America or Europe.

Ancient Times

There is evidence of some milling implements dating to around 2500 BC but although pottery throughout the Americas can be dated from as early as 4000 BC there is no evidence of it being in use in the Argentine lands beyond the Andes until around 500 BC. The peoples of the south were nomadic hunters and fishermen who pursued the game over the empty plains or fished the coastal area.

Only in the north-west, where modern Argentina absorbs the outer reaches of the great Inca Empire of Peru and Bolivia, were there a few hill-top settlements of simple stone construction each housing at most only a few thousand Indians. Here, the populace had a primitive industry in ceramics, copper and bronze-working and even stone sculpture. Life was originated on the basis of a confederation of tribes. The conquest of the area by the Inca armies, around AD 1480 led to the introduction of more sophisticated social organisation, craft-skills, llama herding, improved road communication and irrigation works.

We shall never know how far this advanced Andean civilisation might have spread into the scattered groups of hunter/gatherers of the eastern Andes and Gran Chaco, Pampas and Patagonia. The Conquistadores destroyed the Inca Empire from the Pacific side and soon invaded the last remaining Inca settlements in the Andes and over the into the foothills on the Argentine side. Within only a few decades the first Spaniards arrived at the mouth of the Rio de la Plata, to begin the long, remorseless colonisation of Argentina.

1

300 Years under the Spanish Crown

The name Argentina is a reference to the silver that Spaniards believed was to be found in the area and wanted to ship down the Rio de la Plata (the River of Silver), to the port of Buenos Aires and across the Atlantic to Seville. But what silver was to be found lay in the Andes and was mined and transported down the Pacific side of the mountains to the great port of Lima.

Colonisation spread slowly from Buenos Aires (City of Good Breezes) along the River Plate as the Spaniards searched for mineral wealth, and on into the fertile temperate lands of the Pampas in the centre, up to the Andes mountains in the north and west and down through the semi-desert Patagonian plateau in the south.

Within ten years of the discovery of the Americas by **Columbus**, the man who gave his name to the entire continent, **Americo Vespucci**, was exploring the coast of what are now Brazil, Uruguay and Argentina. Some credit him with the discovery of the River Plate, others award the prize to another explorer, **Juan Díaz de Solís**, who arrived at the mouth of the river in 1516. He must have wished he had not, since shortly afterwards he and some of his crew were captured and killed by Charrua Indians who, according to some accounts,proceeded to eat them before the horrified gaze of the remaining crew aboard ship!

Ferdinand Magellan briefly explored the region in 1520 on his way to the Pacific. A more extensive investigation of the area was undertaken by **Sebastian Cabot** some six years later. Cabot spent three years looking for a legendary mountain of silver before sailing away empty handed. Ten more years were to pass before the first serious colonizing expedition arrived and dropped anchor in the river estuary.

On 3 February, 1536, **Pedro de Mendoza** arrived from Spain with a large fleet of would-be colonists and founded the city of Santa María de los Buenos Aires. The Indians were initially well-disposed towards the early settlers but these newly-arrived colonists, frustrated at not finding the wealth they had imagined, provoked the Indians into attacking the settlement. It

Americo Vespucci

1

Ferdinand Magellan

Sebastian Cabot

Pedro de Mendoza

was a close run thing. The restless Spanish militia, now led by **Domingo Irela**, eventually moved on from Buenos Aires and the banks of the River Plate to found Asunción, today's capital of Paraguay. They never found the mineral riches they imagined to be there. They brought with them, however, the foundation of Argentina's future wealth – cattle and horses.

Almost simultaneously, other Spanish expeditionary forces were entering Argentina from Chile and Peru, crossing the Andean wilderness in search of more Inca treasures. In the process, they founded the great cities of the north-west, Santiago del Estero, Catamarca, Tucumán, Salta, Jujuy, La Rioja and Córdoba. Once conquered, these provinces of what is now Argentina were governed by the Viceroyalty of Peru in Lima and were the most important areas of Spanish activity until the late eighteenth century.

The king of Spain ordered the trade in minerals and other produce of the area to be directed west, through Peru and Panama, back to Spain. Similarly, all goods from Spain were sent through Panama and Peru, ignoring the direct transatlantic route between Seville and Buenos Aires. In 1554 the King went so far as to ban ships using the River Plate altogether.

With no great mineral wealth to encourage immigration, no large indigenous populations to exploit and little interest from Madrid, the small colonial city of Buenos Aires remained an outpost of the Spanish empire. The struggling colony was refounded in 1580, and as late as the 1720s, numbered only some 2,200 inhabitants.

The Viceroyalty of the River Plate

As the Andean mining industries declined and the cost and danger of routing all trade up the Pacific coast and through Panama grew greater, calls for a new Viceroyalty to administer the lands east of the Andes were finally heeded by Madrid. In 1776 the Viceroyalty of the River Plate was proclaimed, with Buenos Aires as its capital. The new Viceroy was responsible for all of Argentina, Paraguay, Uruguay and some areas of south-eastern Peru.

By 1780 the population of Buenos Aires had swelled dramatically to over 35,000, many of mixed Indian and Spanish parentage (since there was a distinct shortage of

1

Spanish ladies prepared to risk the perilous Atlantic crossing to live in what was still a backward and unfashionable part of the empire) and other bonded servants.

Inland from Buenos Aires the **gaucho** culture of the Pampas was spreading rapidly. The *gauchos* were the fiercely self-reliant and sturdy breed of men who tended the herds of cattle being introduced onto the natural pastures of the great Pampas grasslands. *Gauchos* are still revered and romanticised by today's citizens as Argentina's cowboys. If you want to read about their lifestyle try Martín Fierro, a romanticised but well-written account of the *gaucho* legend.

The gauchos

In the north-east, in the Argentine province still known as Missiones, the Jesuits and other missionaries tried to convert and protect the native Indians, with mixed results. At the mercy of greedy Spanish landholders who exploited them for their labour, and succumbing to the devastating European diseases the newcomers brought with them, the native population was catastrophically reduced by the end of the 1800s. Today, only 3 per cent of the population speaks the Indian tongue of Guarani and clings on to life on the very fringes of Argentina in the areas bordering Paraguay and Brazil. Indian populations outside the Andean region and the northeast, always small in number, were particularly devastated.

The Missionaries

Argentina is now almost entirely populated by inhabitants of European origin and those of mixed European and native Indian blood, known as *mestizos*.

Mestizos

The Road to Independence

Once direct trade with Spain was established the agricultural wealth of the hinterlands of Buenos Aires increased dramatically. The newly arrived Spanish immigrants brought new tensions with them. The sons and daughters of the original Spanish settlers, born in Argentina and known as *Criollos* (Creoles), resented the newcomers and resisted the imposition of restrictive direct Spanish rule. The increased trade and shipping with Europe and North America brought a flood of new ideas as well as merchandise into Buenos Aires. Inspired by the success of the American War of Independence and

Criollos

particularly the ideals of the French Revolution, the heavy hand of Spanish imperial government was increasingly resented by the citizens of South America.

King Charles III, an unusually vigorous incumbent of the throne, had angered the colonists by making unpopular reforms which excluded many of mixed blood from lucrative official posts, and introducing a more efficient system of tax collection. When Napoleon Bonaparte invaded Spain and ousted Charles' successor, Ferdinand VII, many in Spanish America saw this as an opportunity to assert their independence while the Spanish Crown was too weak to maintain its grip. Other colonists remained loyal to Spain. War throughout the continent was the inevitable result.

The Battle of Trafalgar

In 1805 **Admiral Nelson** destroyed most of the Spanish (and French) fleet at the Battle of Trafalgar. Without the support of its fleet, the authority of Spain over the restless colonies of the New World was weakened to breaking point. It was not only the restless colonists who saw the opportunity.

The British

In 1806 and again in 1807 a **British expedition** attempted to conquer Buenos Aires. The Spanish Viceroy did not endear himself to the citizens of Buenos Aires by fleeing across the river to Montevideo in Uruguay. The British took the city but were ousted when another great Argentine hero, **Santiago de Liniers**, rallied the remaining Spanish troops and, with the help of the inhabitants, sent the British back to their ships.

Santiago de Liniers

The British did not give up easily. Having taken Montevideo, their army of some 10,000 strong made a second attempt at taking Buenos Aires. Met by Liniers and his combined force of regular soldiers and citizen volunteers, ferocious street battles ensued, which finally convinced the British commander that he would be wiser to sail away with his expeditionary force and leave the city to its redoubtable local inhabitants.

There are few instances in history, apart from the American War of Independence, of a well-equipped British force being so comprehensively sent packing by an improvised and inexperienced citizen militia. The people of Buenos Aires were rightly proud of their efforts and achievements, particularly since their success was not dependent on the protection of the Spanish Crown.

1

As the Iberian Peninsula became increasingly engulfed in chaos, links with the motherland weakened further. The hapless **Ferdinand VII of Spain** was deposed by Bonaparte in an attempt to place his own brother on the Spanish throne. Napoleon's armies swept through Spain in 1808 and the Peninsula descended further into anarchy and civil war. Lord Wellesley (later the Duke of Wellington) and Napoleon's Field Marshals fought a merciless campaign throughout northern and western Spain, leaving the people of the New World without effective imperial government.

Ferdinand VII

In Buenos Aires the citizens convened a *cabildo*, an open town meeting. Swayed by the eloquence and persuasiveness of *Criollo* intellectuals, such as Rivadavia and Belgrano, who had been inspired by the liberalism sweeping through Europe in the wake of the French Revolution, the citizens deposed the Viceroy and declared a revolutionary *junta* to govern in its place.

'Junta' has become a pejorative term, conjuring up images of ambitious military dictators seizing power, but its real sense is of a group combining to organise and oversee affairs. The Junta Directiva of a company in Argentine and throughout the Americas is simply the Board of Directors.

Junta Directiva

1

The May Revolution and Civil War

The new Junta immediately faced opposition from the forces of conservatism in Argentina. The great landowners (*estancieros*), the Church and the Civil Servants sent out by the Spanish Crown saw their privileges threatened by the new liberal regime. Argentine society was split along class, regional and ideological lines as both sides vied for control in the vacuum left by Madrid.

Some wanted to re-establish links with Spain. Although no reinforcements were forthcoming from Europe, substantial Spanish forces still remained in Argentina, Chile and Peru ready to reimpose royal government. Others wanted a strong central government based in Buenos Aires. Yet another powerful group advocated a more Federalist approach, with political power diversified throughout the territory.

Independence

Forcing the issue, the liberals of Buenos Aires declared an autonomous government on 25 May 1810. This is celebrated today as **National Day**, even though formal independence from Spain was not declared until six years later. Although autonomous, Argentina began rapidly to disintegrate. The outlying provinces of what are now Paraguay, Bolivia and Uruguay saw their opportunity to break away. Paraguay gained independence in 1811 and Bolivia was reabsorbed into the Viceroyalty of Peru. The remaining provinces fragmented into smaller, squabbling units under the sway of competing *caudillos* (a term used to describe strong military and political leaders).

Before the Viceroyalty disintegrated entirely, and with Spanish royal armies still active throughout the territory, particularly in the west, a Congress was called at Tucumán in 1816. The fractious provinces agreed to remain together, if only in name, as the United Provinces of the River Plate. It was not to last.

General José de San Martín

The struggle for true independence from Spain engulfed South America from Venezuela to Cape Horn. In Argentina one of the great military heroes of independence, General San Martín, was given the task of clearing the Spanish armies out of Argentina once and for all.

The Liberation of Peru

Revered by the Argentines, San Martín is also a national hero of Chile, which he helped to liberate. From Mendoza, San Martín led his army over the frozen Andes to help Bernardo O'Higgins win the great battles of Chacabuco in 1817 and Maipú in 1818. He was also instrumental in liberating Peru with the help of the Chilean navy and local rebels. Entering Lima in 1821, he declared independence from Spain for the vast Viceroyalty of Peru.

San Martín

After confrontation with that other great liberator of South America, Simón Bolivar, San Martín abandoned South America in 1823 and retired to France where he died in 1850. Although his services to the nation were largely unacknowledged at the time, every town in Argentina now has a street named after him. Long after his death in exile his body was returned to Buenos Aires where it now lies in the Cathedral.

Anarchy, War and Dictatorship (1823-1852)

As the disillusioned San Martín sailed into exile, the government of the United Provinces fell apart. **Bernardino Rivadavia,** the first President of Argentina, tried valiantly to hold the territory together under a strong central government base in Buenos Aires. His efforts to redistribute land and attract more settlers were unsuccessful, largely due to the resistance of the great landowners, who naturally resented the curtailing of their wealth and authority. At the same time, a long-running dispute over the fate of Uruguay degenerated into open warfare with Brazil, which was to last some three years. Rivadavia was forced from office and fled into exile in 1827.

Bernadino Rivadero

With war raging over Uruguay and total anarchy in the interior of the country, where the *caudillos* ruled their great *estancias* as independent fiefdoms, one of the most ruthless strongmen in all South American history rose to power. For the next two decades Argentinian history was dominated by **General Juan Manuel de Rosas**.

General Rosas

1

Rosas was an unusual character. Though born in Buenos Aires he was raised amongst the *gauchos* on his *estancia* on the Pampas. He was a skilled horseman and natural leader, much admired by the simple cowboys, and proved also to be a successful businessman, amassing great wealth and power. In 1829, at the age of 36, he was appointed Governor of the Province of Buenos Aires in the hope that his firm leadership would put an end to the anarchy. The citizens of Buenos Aires got more than they bargained for!

Rosas was the leader of the **Federalist** party, a loose grouping of landowners and regional interests which wanted less central control from Buenos Aires and to be left alone to run their *estancias* without interference. They were opposed by the Unitarists who preferred a more centralised State-controlled rule from Buenos Aires. The Federalists, who chose red for their colours, and the Unitarists, who chose blue, were to fight out a protracted civil war for the soul of the nation for the next two decades.

Federalists and Unitarists

At first the Federalists had the upper hand and Rosas signed the **Federal Pact** in 1831 uniting the Provinces of

Buenos Aires, Entre Rios, Corrientes and Santa Fé together on an equal footing. At the end of his first term as Governor in 1832 Rosas was refused the almost dictatorial powers he demanded to continue in office. Disgusted, he took himself off to Patagonia where he fought a merciless war of virtual extermination against the primitive Indian population still living there.

The Desert Campaign

It was during this **Desert Campaign** (1833-34), as it is known, that Rosas met Charles Darwin. The great scientist was favourably impressed with the energy and authority of the Argentine General. He recorded the following incident in his diary:

> 'A man a short time since murdered another; being arrested and questioned he answered: "the man spoke disrespectfully of General Rosas and I killed him". In one week's time the murderer was at liberty'.

While Rosas campaigned against the Patagonian Indians his wife, Doña Encarnación, remained in Buenos Aires to make life difficult for the three hapless Governors who succeeded her husband. She was by all accounts as ambitious and ruthless as he, an Argentinian Lady Macbeth who would stop at nothing to help Rosas seize power. In 1835 she achieved the result she had schemed so hard for and the Junta re-appointed her husband Governor, this time with the unfettered authority he demanded. With the backing of the Federalists *caudillos* and their *gauchos* his power over Argentina was total, and he set out to eliminate all effective opposition in a reign of systematic oppression of all dissent.

For years the *caudillos* and the *gauchos* dispensed rough justice to control the great expanses of the interior of Argentina. Parallels with the American Wild West are not unjustified, but the *caudillos* demonstrated an appetite for cruelty unknown to their northern neighbours. The more fortunate opponents had their property seized and suffered only exile or imprisonment. Castration and the cutting out of tongues were not unknown. The really unlucky ones were murdered, often by having their throats cut or their bodies skewered with *gaucho* lances. Executed Unitarists were strung up in the Plaza de Mayo outside the President's residence, mockingly dressed in the blue colours of their party and with a placard around their neck reading 'Fresh Meat' or 'Beef still in its hide'.

1

Rosas provided a cloak of legitimacy to these abusive ways. He continued his attempts to exert full control over Uruguay with little success and his xenophobia led to a drain of foreign capital from the young nation. Outside investment dried up and few immigrants were willing to risk their lives in such an atmosphere. Relationships with England and France were so bad that these two nations, which only a few decades before had fought the Napoleonic wars, organised a joint blockade of the River Plate, bringing the Argentine economy to its knees.

If you walk through the centre of Buenos Aires or any other major Argentine city today you will see the same street names – Rivadavia, Sarmiento, Mitre, Alberdi, Urquiza – names of the liberal intellectuals and men of action who inspired the secret opposition to Rosas. An uprising in 1852, led by Urquiza, resulted in the decisive battle of Caseros, just outside Buenos Aires. Rosas was defeated and exiled. He spent the last 25 years of his life in the quiet provincial port of Southampton in England – a strange choice for such a xenophobic, nationalistic son of the Pampas.

The Constitution of 1853 and the Development of the Nation State

Argentine's present constitution is a direct descendant of the document produced at the convention held at Santa Fé in 1853. The new **Constitution of the Republic** was proclaimed on 1 May and **Urquiza** elected as the President. Although Buenos Aires was the political centre of the Republic, it was not officially the capital. Power was divided between the increasingly wealthy port of Buenos Aires and Paraná further inland. This division of administrative and political power was finally resolved after a Congress in 1862 which recognised Buenos Aires as the provincial capital of the River Plate region and of the whole Republic.

Urquiza's Presidency was marked by consolidation in the fields of banking, education and transportation. This solid work was continued by his successor, **Bartolomé Mitre**, despite the outbreak of the most protracted war in the region to date. From 1865 to 1870 it took the Triple Alliance of Argentina, Brazil and Uruguay to curb and

General Rosas

1

Bartolomé Mitre

finally subdue the aggressive ambitions of the Paraguayan dictator Francisco Solano López. The cost in lives and wealth was massive, leaving Paraguay a shrivelled and weakened relic of its former self. Argentina consolidated its control of the provinces of Formosa, Missiones and Chaco.

Domingo Sarmiento

During the war with Paraguay an orderly transition of power in Buenos Aires saw **Domingo Faustino Sarmiento** elected successor to Mitre in 1868. Sarmiento is regarded as the father of the modern Argentine education system. He also presided over a period of increased European immigration to Argentina which saw the city of Buenos Aires in particular swell to an economic importance and political weight which would settle all doubts as to the capital once and for all.

Avellaneda

Although Mitre tried to prevent the succession of **Avellaneda** to the Presidency at the end of Sarmiento's mandate in 1874 by leading a short-lived rebellion, the next President continued the consolidation of the state institutions and transportation systems begun under Sarmiento.

Julio Roca

The few Indians who still clung to life in the remote regions of Patagonia were subjected to yet worse treatment by Avellaneda's Minister of War, **General Julio Roca**, (another name to be seen everywhere on streets signs in Argentina). He went on to be President of the Republicfor most of the decade Although thousands more square kilometres were opened for settlement in the south few chose to leave the comfortable life of an increasingly affluent Buenos Aires region.

The Golden Years (1880-1914)

In the three decades spanning the end of the nineteenth and the beginning of the twentieth centuries, Argentina prospered in a way remembered as a golden period in its history. Immigrants continued to flood in from Europe – mainly from Spain, Italy, Ireland and Germany but also from Switzerland, France and almost any other European country you can think of. By 1910, three-quarters of the citizens of Buenos Aires had been born in Europe.

The biggest boom was in agriculture. The population of the Pampas grew; yet more railways were needed to bring the produce to Buenos Aires, and refrigeration plants required to store the meat. The British poured money into Argentina. One-third of all British investment in Latin America in the last decades of the nineteenth century went into building railways in Argentina, carrying Argentine beef, wool, mutton and grain to the docksides, where they were loaded into British vessels for the transatlantic crossing.

The end of the war saw a collapse in demand for Argentine raw materials. The main markets for Argentine goods, Britain, France and Germany, were all exhausted. For the first, but far from the last, time strikes were called, paralysing the economy. Already dependent on collapsing economies, the country struggled to repay foreign debt and for the first time in its history Argentina began to import more than it could export. With the immigrants came new political ideas. Unions were organised and socialism spread throughout the working classes.

The spread of Socialism

The government of the Radical Civil Union, led on and off by Hipólito Irigoyen from 1916 until 1930 met increasingly restless strikers with repression. President Irigoyen had maintained a strictly neutral stance throughout the First World War but as the war ended and recession began to bite, the workers became increasingly restless and frustrated at the lack of political progress towards democracy in Argentina. In 1919 troops opened fire on strikes in the streets, killing many. Argentines refer to the event as the *Semana Trágica* (Tragic Week).

Semana Trágica

The Great Depression following the crash of 1929 badly affected the Argentine economy as exports to the suddenly impoverished and turmoil stricken markets in Europe and North America shrank. The second great wave of immigrants who had fled war-torn Europe could not be absorbed entirely into the now faltering Argentine economy. Industry had always been relatively underdeveloped and could not offer full employment for the many poor immigrants thronging the streets of Buenos Aires. The civilian government of the day – along with most governments around the world at this time – did not know how to cope with the situation.

As the helplessness and unpopularity of the civilian government grew, the frustrated military deposed Irigoyen in what was to be the first of many interventions in the government of Argentina.

1

During the 1930s Argentine politics became a maelstrom of intrigue and corruption. Civilian governments came and went. Some efforts were made to clean up the system, particularly by President **Ortiz**, before he died in office and was succeeded by President **Castillo**, a man with strong pro-Axis sympathies and so inept that he triggered another military coup in 1943. With the Second World War raging, Argentina found itself yet again under military dictatorship. This time it was to have more dramatic consequences, since from the ranks of the military emerged a man who was to shape the destiny of the nation for decades to come – **Juan Domingo Perón.**

Ortiz and Castillo

General Juan Perón, Evita Duarte and Peronismo

Juan Perón was an ambitious military officer who had risen to prominence in 1943 as Minister of Labour and Social Welfare. The post was regarded by his fellow military officers as unimportant, but Colonel Perón used it to gain support and build the most powerful political machine Argentina has ever seen. In 1944 he became Defence Minister and shortly thereafter Vice-President to General Farrell, the third military President since President Castillo had been forced to resign in June 1943. One President, General Rawson, had only lasted two days!

Perón was not a member of the traditional Argentine military and social élite. His period as a military observer in Italy under Mussolini had shown him the power to be gained by manipulating the masses through organising labour on political as well as union lines. He was a Nationalist, not a Fascist, but he learned well from the Fascist's political techniques for organising support amongst the masses. Throughout the war, Perón strengthened his hold on power. and organised the *descamisados* (shirtless ones), an organisation drawn from the lower classes. In February 1946, after a populist campaign laced with strong nationalist and anti-American rhetoric, the votes of his organised supporters propelled him to the Casa Rosada as President.

Together with his charismatic wife, Eva Duarte, he controlled the destiny of Argentina until his exile to Madrid in the early 1950s, and continued to influence and manipulate the politics of his homeland until his Beardwooddeath in 1974.

Perón is still either idolised or reviled in Argentina. The traditional political parties, long in the hands of conservative landowners and wealthy magnates, were swept aside. Péron pursued a vigorous policy of nationalisation of all major foreign companies and encouraged locally capitalised industrial expansion. The urban workers were wooed by the introduction of an ambitious and generous social security system coupled with housing and health reforms.

But the Argentine economy faltered as bad weather affected the harvests and prices for grain on the international market plummeted. The weakness of the Argentine dependence on agricultural exports, despite Perón's attempts to diversify into industry, was exposed yet again. With fewer exports worth less, the national debt grew out of control and Perón faced severe economic and financial problems which put the maintenance of his expensive welfare reforms in doubt.

Worse was to befall the beleaguered President. Unbeknown to the Argentinc people, his wife was dying of cancer. **Evita** was elevated almost to sainthood by the adoring 'shirtless ones' whom she courted through astute use of the newspapers, radio and mass rallies. Her Foundation distributed huge amounts of money and food in a haphazard but headline-grabbing manner throughout her husband's Presidency.

Evita was much more than a populist rabblerouser. Her own background (born illegitimate in a provincial backwater) enabled her to understand the needs of the poor. Her rags to riches story endeared her to them. Though snubbed by Argentine high society and ridiculed for her dazzling clothes and jewellery, the people loved her blatant display of wealth and power. But, no mindless mannequin riding to fame on the back of her husband's office, Evita had a political acumen which Perón relied upon.

Although the allegiance of the masses lay with the Peróns, the wealthy middle class and armed forces, particularly the navy, were never truly behind the radical experiments of the populist government. The early death of Evita, from uterine cancer in 1952, signalled the beginning of the end for the Perón government. Without her, the policies of his regime began to unravel, leading to

1

Evita

inflation, widespread business failures and unemployment. By 1955 the situation had become critical.

Perón refused to face the financial crisis and continued his grandiose spending and profligate ways. Seizing their opportunity, his opponents in the airforce and navy led a coup, bombing the Casa Rosada. The army opposed the coup and the nation teetered on the brink of civil war. Enraged Peronist supporters burned down churches in revenge for what they saw as the Church's role in fomenting opposition to the President. Perón fled to Paraguay and finally settled in Madrid.

Perón may have departed but the problems remained, a deadly legacy for all who succeeded him. It was as if the Casa Rosada had a revolving front door, as nine Presidents came and went during the eighteen years between Perón's exile and return. One President, Arturo Frondizi, suffered some 30 attempted coups against his government!

1

Evita

Although the popular image of Evita outside Argentina is one of a woman adored by all, the reality is that you will meet many Argentines who do not hold to that view. Many, particularly the children of the middle class who saw their family wealth confiscated, destroyed by catastrophic economic policies and their social position undermined, regard the Peronist years as a disaster. To most Argentine's however she is still a revered figure, respected for her achievements in obtaining the vote women and providing real help in housing, health and education for the poor.

As Perón's successors became ever more repressive, the military more brutal, and the economy more unstable, the Peronists gained ground with the masses and the stage was set for his return.

In 1973 the Peronist Party competed in presidential elections and won. **Hector Cámpora** formed a government and invited Perón to return to Argentina. He was greeted at Ezeiza airport by a crowd estimated at over two million.

Emotions ran high, fights broke out between rival demonstrators and a pitch battle evolved between the crowd and the security forces leaving hundreds dead. Cámpora, who many regarded as a Perón stooge anyway, resigned. This necessitated another Presidential election, which Perón won easily in October 1973. He returned to the Casa Rosada after almost two decades in exile, with his new wife Maria Estela (known as **Isabelita**) at his side as his Vice-President, an unusual arrangement by anyones political standards!

Perón was already an old and ailing man when he assumed the Presidency for the second time. He died in office on July 1st 1974, leaving his wife Isabelita to succeed him.

Isabelita was no second Evita. She had none of the political intelligence, strength and charisma of her predecessor and presided over a descent into corruption, anarchy and economic meltdown. Inflation was rampant, a full scale guerrilla war was being fought out in the streets of Argentine cities and the nation was in the hands of one of perhaps the most incompetent governments Latin America has ever seen. Isabelita relied heavily on sycophantic cronies, especially a dark character called López Rega, who played Rasputin to her bewildered, frightened Empress. The economy was a shambles, the government bereft of any ideas or competence. It was to the relief of almost everyone that the military finally lost patience and packed her off into exile in March 1976. A Perón left the Casa Rosada, this time for ever.

La Guerra Sucia (The Dirty War) 1976-1982

The succession of military Juntas which ruled Argentina until their defeat at the hands of the British in 1982 in the Mavinas conflict turned out to be one of the most ruthless regimes known to modern history. They abolished the Congress and all Latin American forms of democratic expression were dismantled or very strictly controlled. Those openly opposed to the government were often murdered or imprisoned – only the lucky ones escaped into exile. Opponents were kidnapped and disappeared. Some were thrown, still alive, out of military aircraft flying over the Atlantic. Whole families were arrested.

Perón's Successors

Isabelita

1

Some were tortured mercilessly in special prisons before being killed. Children of leftwingers were taken from their families and given to childless military families. Children, as young as five or seven years old, were even dumped alone at night on the streets of neighbouring Chilean cities. Fear was way of life for many Argentines.

General Videla and his successor **General Viola** proved remarkably deaf to pleas for clemency from outside Argentina. Inside Argentina the famous **Mothers of the Plaza de Mayo** protested every Thursday by walking around the square in front of the Casa Rosada wearing white headscarves and demanding to know what had happened to their loved ones. They too were ignored.

Mothers of the Plaza de Mayo

But what could not be ignored was the rampant inflation which was tearing the Argentine economy to pieces. Money became worthless, bankruptcies increased and the foreign debt became totally unmanageable. The heavily protected Argentine industry continued producing obsolete cars, televisions and fridges, etc. that even the Argentines did not want to buy. Any imported goods became an expensive luxury. The middle classes were becoming sick of the repression and economic mismanagement.

The Malvinas (Falklands) War

Incapable of righting the economy or continuing their repression, the military hit on the desperate measure of attempting to retake the Malvinas (Falkland Islands) from the British by force. Patriotism is the last refuge of a scoundrel and the military régime, now under **General Galtieri**, had no other option. The war was immensely popular in Argentina and initially the Argentine forces had some spectacular successes taking the islands with little effort and gambling that the British would accept the invasion as a *faît accompli*. But Galtieri miscalculated.

General Galtieri

The British under Mrs.Thatcher reacted with determination. A Task Force set sail for the South Atlantic to retake the islands. Argentine forces, mostly poorly trained and ill-equiped conscripts from the provinces, were no match for a professional army. The Argentine navy was neutralised after their flagship the *Belgrano* was sunk by a British submarine. The

The sinking of the Belgrano

1

Argentine airforce performed well, sinking several Royal Navy ships, notably HMS *Sheffield*. The British land forces quickly and efficiently put an end to all Argentine resistance on the islands and forced a complete surrender on the Argentine military.

The Argentine public became aware mid-way through their conflict that their military leaders had been exaggerating their successes in the Malvinas. As the realisation of impending defeat sank in disillusionment with the military became complete. Galtieri was unceremoniously removed by his fellow officers but their next Presidential nominee, a retired officer untainted by the Malvinas débacle, **General Bignone**, was equally ineffectual at tackling the country's woes. Inflation hit over 400 per cent and demonstrations for a return to democracy grew in size and strength.

General Bignone

Bignone had little choice but to allow general elections in 1983 to restore civilian government. On 10 December 1983 the military Junta dissolved itself and President **Raúl Alfonsín** of the Radical Party was handed the unenviable task of restoring democratic constitutional government to an exhausted and dispirited nation. Few thought he would survive his term in office without facing another military coup.

Raúl Alfonsín

1

Raúl Alfonsín

Before leaving office the Bignone Junta passed a law generously absolving all officers for any crimes committed during the Dirty War. But if they thought that they could walk away from their murderous acts unpunished they were mistaken. The first act of the new President was to repeal the amnesty. Courageously **President Alfonsín** had the military leaders, including ex-Presidents Videla and Viola, arrested and tried for human rights violations. They received long prison sentences, life in the cases of General Videla and Admiral Massera, but were allowed to serve their time in the comfort and security of luxuriously equipped military prisons.

Attempts to bring to trial the more junior officers of the régime who had perpetrated the tortures and killings proved less successful. There were several minor garrison uprisings and the government increasingly feared the possibility of a full scale military uprising. They backed down from prosecuting this level of officers and produced a controvertial **Law of Due Obedience** which in effect exonerated junior officers on the grounds that they were only obeying orders. Throughout his presidency Alfonsín battled to avoid further bloodshed and to heal the deep wounds in Argentine society, although he was only partially successful.

The years after the fall of the Junta saw a swing towards liberalism unprecedented in Argentine history. Censorship was abolished, free speech flourished and the people of Argentina were free to indulge their passion for argument and debate in such previously forbidden areas as abortion, contraception, divorce and social reform. The arts flourished, particularly cinema. Many returned from exile as the nation slowly returned to normalcy and democracy.

The swing towards liberalism

Alfonsín announced a new currency, the Austral, which was worth 1,000 old pesos. Wages and prices were frozen and some austerity measures in government spending were implemented. To everyone's surprise these unpalatable measures were broadly accepted by the nation and had an immediate effect in reducing the rampant hyper-inflation.

But Alfonsín was preoccupied with the problems of what to do with the accused from the military of the Dirty War, so the economy began to deteriorate again, unemployment rose and inflation crept up to 200 per cent a month. It was a country in economic turmoil which Alfonsín handed to the next President. Worn out, he voluntarily handed over the Presidency a few months before the end of his full term in office. Had he decided to stay in office he would have been the first president to serve a full term in over a quarter of a century. He remains an active and respectful figure in Argentine politics today.

Carlos Menem

After a peaceful and fair general election President Alfonsín placed the ceremonial sky blue and white sash of the Presidency over the shoulder of **Carlos Menem**, leader of the Peronist party in May 1989. This transition of power from one civilian government to the next was a moment of triumph for the forces of democracy and constitutionalism in Argentina.

Menem was a popular former Governor of La Rioja province with a glamorous image, filmstar hairdo and a simple but effective electoral message – he would remove the freeze on wages. The electoral promise worked and this former truck driver who had gone on to be a distinguished lawyer and who had been imprisoned during the Dirty War, found himself head of the Argentine nation. He promptly reneged on his promises and embarked on free market policies.

Unrepentant junior military officers continued to cause trouble. In December 1990 a group known as the *Carapintadas*, by virtue of their habit of painting their face with camouflage paints, rose in open rebellion. They seized the Argentine army headquarters near the Casa Rosada and other key installations in Buenos Aires. It was futile. The public looked upon them with contempt and their own senior officers were not going to surrender military authority and power to their juniors. Although the rebellion ended peacefully, it was nevertheless proof of the continuing volatility of Argentine politics and society.

Menem pressed on with reform at breathtaking speed. In an effort to attract the foreign investment Argentina so desperately needed. He sold off ailing state industries at knockdown prices disregarding for the interests of the over-cossetted but underpaid workers in them. The Austral currency unit was scrapped and replaced by the Peso, pegged to the US dollar.

1

Menem's Reforms

The 200% monthly inflation he had inherited began to come down but at great cost to the tens of thousands of workers who found themselves ousted from what they thought were jobs for life in the state industries, and the owners of over 10,000 businesses who went under when Menem scrapped Argentina's stiff tariffs on imported goods. Unemployment rose to a previously unthinkable 20 per cent. Bank interest rates remained high as he squeezed the remaining inflation out of the economy. For Argentines life was suddenly tough, but they could see progress and at least the government was taking a strong lead.

With many Argentines facing unemployment, insecurity and reduced purchasing power by the time Menem came up for re-election in 1995, it is a testament to Argentine fear of inflation that he was returned to office.

Recent Leadership

Menem achieved a little under half of the popular vote but it was enough to see off his divided opponents who had failed to come up with any convincing economic policies other than the bitter medicine Menem had prescribed.

One of Menem's achievements has been to curb the power of the great Trade Unions by introducing new labour laws which have swept away much of Perón's protectionist legacy of the welfare state. Argentina is now much more of a 'hire and fire' economy than it was in the first three quarters of the last century. Job insecurity is now no longer a novelty for many Argentines.

The military have seen the end of compulsory conscription, a reduced budget and a diminished role in Argentina's internal affairs. On the other hand Menem has reduced the restlessness of his military leaders by leaving the Non-Aligned Pact, moving closer to the United States and encouraging Argentine military participation in United Nations peacekeeping responsibilities. Good relations with the British have been restored and the nation finds itself at peace again with itself and welcomed back into the fraternity of democratic countries.

President Fernando De La Rua – President today

In October 1999 Fernando De La Rua of the Alliance party won the election as President with 49 per cent of the vote. Only 40 per cent is needed to avoid a second ballot of the top two candidates. The Alliance party also won control of 16 of the 19 provinces in terms of seats but they do not have outright control of the Congress. The Justicialist Party (the Peronist and Menem party) retained a majority in the Senate and still provides over half the Provincial governors.

1

exploring the
potential market

exploring the
potential market

The business traveller should be as well informed as possible before entering a new market. This section acts as a guide to where to find this information. It includes government and private sources in electronic and hardcopy format, and discusses the availability of reliable market and economic information.

Whether you are visiting Argentina for the first time or making the latest in a series of regular visits preparation is essential to get the most out of the trip and ensure that your project succeeds. Obtaining the latest information will allow you to plan effectively for your trip, get a clear picture of the market you are entering, identify any trends or opportunities that you can use to your advantage and spot any possible pitfalls. It is equally important to ensure that the information you use is accurate and that you are aware of any possible bias.

The sources below provide a starting point for research on the Argentina market. Many of them are free or provide information at very little cost.

Argentine Embassies

US
1600 New Hampshire Avenue NW,
Washington DC 20009
❏ Tel: +1 202 939 6400; fax: +1 202 238 6471

Consulates in Atlanta, Chicago, Los Angeles, Miami, New York and San Francisco.

UK
65 Brook Street, London W1K 4AH
❏ Tel: +44 20 7318 1300; fax: +44 20 7318 1301/ 20 7318 1331

US Ministries and other Government Agencies

The US State Department and the Department of Commerce provide a wide range of information to US companies operating in Argentina, including the *Country Commercial Guide*, a comprehensive look at the business environment in Argentina. This is naturally biased towards US business but much of the information is more generally applicable. The *Country Commercial Guides* can be downloaded from the Internet at:
[www.state.gov/about_state/business/com_guides/index].

Export Assistance Center

Specific information and Support

The specific start point for any US company wishing to consider doing business in Latin America would be to approach their local US Export Assistance Center of the International Trade Administration, US and Foreign Commercial Service of the US Department of Commerce. (*See* Appendix 3.)

Trade Information Center, International Trade Administration

US Department of Commerce
Washington DC 20230
❑ Tel: +1 800 USA TRADE; fax: +1 202 482 4473
E-mail: TIC@ita.doc.gov
Website: [www.ita.doc.gov/TICFrameset]

This website contains a directory of trade contacts at the federal, state and local levels for US exporters. The directory can be viewed by state, division and zip code.

Military Sales

The Bureau of Export Administration's Office of Strategic Industries and Economic Security provides defence market research, analysis and technology reports, business opportunities, and advocacy assistance for foreign military sales.

US Department of Commerce
Room 3876 BXA
14th and Constitution Ave. NW
Washington DC 20230
❑ Tel: +1 202 482 4060;
Website: [www.bxa.doc.gov/OSIES]

UK Ministries and other Government Agencies

Trade Partners UK

The primary British government source for information on overseas markets is **Trade Partners UK** which brings the export promotion activities of the Department of Trade and Industry (DTI) and Foreign and Commonwealth Office (FCO) into one new organisation. It acts as a first point of contact for market and business information and it produces a suite of publications ranging from introductory guides to specialist literature on agency law, etc. and offers a variety of services to small and medium sized companies wanting to break into new markets. These services include financial support for official trade missions and UK groups attending key exhibitions.

Much of the information held is available on the Trade Partners website at [www.tradepartners.gov.uk]

Argentine is covered as part of the Southern Cone Unit:

Kingsgate House
66-74 Victoria Street
London SW1E 6SW
❑ Tel: +44 20 7215 4329/4891; fax: +44 20 7215 4831

Through its **Gateway Information Centre,** Trade Partners UK provides information and advice direct to UK business. The Information Centre is a research facility available to exporters and their representatives wishing to undertake their own export market research. It provides access to a comprehensive collection of overseas market information, foreign economic and commercial statitics, trade and telephone directories (as publications, CD-ROMs or Internet databases), mail-order catalogues, and information on the multilateral development agencies including projects and initiatives which they are funding. Access is free. For further information contact:
❑ Tel: +44 20 2175 5444; fax: +44 20 7215 4231 or e-mail [emic@xpd3.dti.gov.uk]

The **Export Market Information Research Service** (EMIRS) provides a fee-based research service based in the information centre for exporters and their representatives. These facilities are based at the same address above.

EMIRS

Another free source of assistance is Trade Partners UK's Export Promoters. In 1995 the then Secretary for State for Industry, Michael Heseltine, and his Minister for Trade, Richard Needham, launched an initiative to promote British exports. They proposed to second up to 100 people from British Industry who were specialists either in certain countries or certain disciplines. These Export Promoters (EPs) are seconded to Trade Partners UK from British Industry for a period of up to three years. The majority of these experts are businessmen with particular knowledge of specific countries. In a few cases the promoter is an

Export Promoters

industry specialist (e.g. environment, power, etc.). Export Promoters are available to everyone. They are likely to be frequent visitors to their countries of responsibility and will have information relating to opportunities, agents, partners, exhibitions, trade missoions, etc. They can generally be found through the Country Manager at Trade Partners UK in Kingsgate House, although they may not often be in that office as many either work from home or are attached to one of the regional Trade Partners offices. These EPs are not only expected to be well-informed but are also likely to be candid about their markets and the opportunities for a particular company. They will usually be able to provide companies with introductions and contacts at the highest level. They have a reporting line directly to the Minister for Trade in the UK. Outside the UK they work closely with the Commercial section of the relevant Embassy.

Since Export Promoters are, through the nature of their secondment, likely to change regularly, it is best to contact the office above to get the currernt EPs contact details. There is, however, normally one EP focused specifically on the Mercosur region.

Trade UK.com

Another key feature of Trade Partners support for the exporting community is TradeUK.com, a unique facility for finding new markets overseas. TradeUK.com is an internet-based service designed to match British exporters with international opportunities. It is free and open to everyone, anywhere, 24 hours a day 365 days a year. TradeUK.com can help companies in two ways:

National Exporters Database

Firstly, they can register, free of charge, on the National Exporters Database. On registration, a company's details are placed on the internet, allowing overseas companies to find them through accessing the database, which is widely advertised abroad. It is also possible to engineer a direct link to companies' own websites. Currently, over 55,000 companies are registered.

Export Sales Leads Service

Secondly, companies can save time, money and effort by using the Export Sales Leads Service to obtain international sales leads. This service offers hot business leads from Trade Partners UK's global network of staff based in the Commercial Sections of British Embassies and Consulates-General. These leads are matched to company requirements and e-mailed directly to the company. The types of lead are many – specific private sector opportunities, tenders and public sector oppportunities, joint-venture and cooperation oppportunities and multilateral aid oppportunities. It is also possible to access market pointers showing trends around the world, and direct entries from overseas companies. For further information go to [www.tradeuk.com] or ❏ Tel: +44 20 7925 7810; fax +44 20 7925 7770 or e-mail [export@brightstation.com].

The Business Link network is a series of one-stop shops designed to meet local export and business requirements. All Business Links offer access to an Export Development Counsellor (EDC) who can assist with export related issues. For details of your nearest Business Link ❏ tel: +44 345 567765 or visit the Business Link Signpost website at [www.businesslink.co.uk]

Business Link

Scotland: Scottish Trade International,
❏ Tel: +44 9141 228 2812/2808 or [www.sti.org.uk]
Wales: Welsh Office Overseas Trade Services,
❏ Tel: +44 1222 825 097 or [www,wales.gov.uk]
Northern Ireland: Industrial Development Board for Northern Ireland,
❏ Tel: +44 2890 233233 or [www.idbni.co.uk]

2

Credit Guarantees

ECGD or the **Export Credits Guarantee Department** is a government department reporting to the Minister for Trade. The ECGD exists primarily to insure export finance. Typically, a project is structured through the banking system, with ECGD providing a guarantee to the financing bank against default for commercial or political reasons. Argentina occasionally makes use of this type of financing.

ECGD

One of the most common ways in which ECGD becomes involved with an export is through a line of credit. When a UK bank offers a facility to an overseas bank to enable goods or services to be purchased from the UK, ECGD can insure that risk. The loan facility is used to pay the exporter once the goods have been exported or the service performed. If the borrower fails to repay any part of the loan, the UK bank is covered by the ECGD guarantee. Overseas investment insurance is also available, offering protection for joint-venture or equity investment abroad.

2

ECGD
PO Box 2200
2 Exchange Tower
Harbour Exchange Square
London E14 9GS
❑ Tel: +44 20 7512 7000

There are a number of private sector companies which offer insurance against default on export contracts – for example NCM and Trade Indemnity.

Military Sales

DESO

Advice on military sales and equipment can be obtained from a specialist organisation in London, the Defence Export Sales Organisation (DESO), part of the Ministry of Defence. This is a very active export service manned by senior diplomats on temporary secondment to DESO. The business is highly specialised and is handled by the defence attachés rather than by the embassy commercial offices. Defence sales include obvious military hardware and equipment and also takes in the construction of airfields, supply of 4x4 vehicles and uniforms, etc. DESO will also advise on any local political sensitivities.

DESO
Ministry of Defence
Metropole Building
Northumberland Avenue, London WC2N 5BL
❑ Tel: +44 20 7218 9000; fax: +44 20 7807 8307

Other Ministries

British Council

The task of promoting cultural and educational enterprises and exports is actively undertaken by the **British Council**. The Council, with offices across the UK, is financially self-supporting and is embracing the world of commerce with increasing vigour and imagination. It has offices responsible for exports and for liaison with other government bodies, in particular Trade Partners UK. The British Council has offices in Buenos Aires and is very active. Although still widely associated with its general promotion of British culture and the English language and thus perhaps thought irrelevant to hardcore business, the Council is a leading proponent for the UK education and human resource development sector.

Contact details for the British Council in Argentina are:

MT Alvear
590 4th floor
1058 Buenos Aires
❏ Tel: (11) 4311 9814; fax: (11) 4311 7745

British Council in the UK:
❏ Tel: +44 20 7930 8466; website: [www.britcoun.org]
or [newweb.britcoun.org]

Two other ministries which promote British exports are
the **Ministry of Agriculture** and **The Department of the
Environment, Transport and the Regions** (DETR). The
export departments in these ministries have specialised
information freely available to businessmen and women.
Overseas visits by ministries and officials accompanied
by business people are frequently arranged.

Ministry of Agriculture: [www.maff.gov.uk]
DETR: [www.detr. gov.uk]

In general, all UK government offices can be found at
[www.open.gov.uk] or use the excellent *Civil Service
Yearbook* produced by the Cabinet Office and published
by the Stationary Office: ❏ Tel: +44 870 600 5522.

**Ministry of
Agriculture**

DETR

2

The European Union

The relevant office of the European Union (EU) is
Directorate General 1 (DG1) which deals with trade and
political matters; it is based in Brussels and also has
overseas representative offices. DG1 also controls the
European Community Investment Partners scheme
(ECIP), finance for the region and relations with the
European Investment Bank (EIB). DG1 has country
desks, much the same as Trade Partners UK and the FCO,
with desk officers, who offer information and assistance.

Funds are available from the European Union for various
development programmes other than direct project
finance, including finance for companies to set up
partnerships and/or joint ventures. The ECIP scheme can
assist with finance to form such a joint venture and for
training of personnel. ECIP can also finance feasibility
studies prior to a joint venture agreement.

Further assistance and advice can be obtained from
various other sources, such as the commercial section of
the **United Kingdom Permanent Representation**

45

UKRep

(UKRep) office in Brussels, which exists to assist British companies to understand and participate in the programmes administered by the European Institutions in Brussels. The British-Argentina Chamber of Commerce in London can also offer advice on the maze of Brussels. Registration with Brussels is essential for consultants. Manufacturers with specialised products should also pre-qualify to participate in EU funded projects.

Australia

The Australian Trade Commision, or Austrade, is the federal governments export and investment facilitation agency. Austrade provides advice to Australian companies on general export issues, assistance in determining which overseas markets hold potential for their products and aid in building a presence in the market. Through their network of global offices, Austrade can assist with finding potental business partners or agents, prepare publicity material, organise product launches and offer assistance with attending suitable exhibitions. If Austrade cannot help with your specific requirement, they will direct you to an appropriate government or private service which can.

Austrade

2

Austrade Online is an enhanced website facility at [www.austrade.gov.au] which provides up to date reference points regarding international trade issues and export programmes. Australian companies can also take out a free listing within the website allowing inclusion on a searchable database of products and services.

Under their **Export Market Development Grant** (EMDG) scheme, Austrade may be able to reimburse eligible businesses for part of their export marketing costs.

Further Sources of Information

LATAG

This is a Trade Partners UK advisory group for Latin America whose main purpose is to assist in the formulation of government trade policy and to seek out and promote ways of improving UK performance in the region, acting as an interface between industry and government. Its staff can provide briefing for UK firms and can advise on more specialised information sources available to the exporter.

2 Belgrave Square
London SW1X 8PJ
❑ Tel: +44 20 7235 2303; fax: +44 20 7235 3581
Website: [www.latag.com]

The British Argentine Chamber of Commerce
BACC is responsible for mutual trade and economic
interests through meetings, exhibitions and publications.
A regular journal is published free and is available to
those interested.

BACC
2 Belgrave Square
London SW1X 8PJ
❑ Tel: +44 20 7245 6661; fax: +44 20 7 235 7013
E-mail: [bims@abccbims.force9.co.uk]

Chambers of Commerce or any trade or professional
body to which you belong may be able to provide
information on Argentina. They may not produce the
material themselves, but should have a library where
such information is held. These bodies may also ask for a
fee to research on your behalf. This is more costly, but
saves time – to make the most of the service, be specific
in defining your research project.

Some Chambers in the UK have developed good links with
Argentina through trade missions: North Derbyshire,
Liverpool, Birmingham and London, for example.

The Internet
As is the case with all the World Wide Web, there are
good, bad, up-to-date and horribly dated sites. Some
pages related to Argentina are:

Media:
Reuters	[www.reuters.com]
Clarín	[www.clarin.com]
La Nación	[www.lanacion.com]
Ambito Financiero	[www.ambito.com]
El Cronista	[www.cronista.com]
Buenos Aires Herald	[www.buenosairesherald.com]

Official Argentine reference:
Ministerio Economía	[www.mecon.ar]
Centro De Economía	[http:\\ccimreric.gov\indi.htm]
Boletín Oficial	[www.jus.gov.ar/servi/boletin]

2

INDEC	[www.indec.mecon.ar]
Mercosur	[www.guia-mercosur.com]
Boletín Mercosur	[www.argarnet.com]
Laws/resolutions etc.	[www.infoleg.mecon.ar]
Directorio Argentino	[www.grippo.com]

Business:

Business Trends	[www.tendencies.com.ar]
Guía de la Industria	[www.guiaindustria.com.ar]
Mercosur Export	[www.mercosurexport.com]
Trade Fairs Calendar	[www.feriasycongresos.com.ar]
Hotels in Argentina	[www.guiahotelera.com.ar]
LATAG	[www.latag.com]

Digging Deeper

Once you have an overview of the market, you may want more detailed economic information or wish to concentrate on your particular sector. This is where the cost of research starts to increase – but you will be very well informed and the risk of unpleasant surprises later on will be much reduced. You will be aware of the trends and the possible effects on your business and therefore able to plan for them.

Economic and Country Guides

Two of the best sources of detailed economic information and analysis are **Dun & Bradstreet** (D&B) and the **Economist Intelligence Unit** (EUI). D&B offer an authorative web-based information service which includes data on most markets. The D&B Country Risk Service delivers comprehensive information sources for evaluating risk and opportunities. Their approach is to combine constant monitoring with an archive service on a wide range of topics. Most companies can qualify for a 14-day free trial period. D&B also offer two excellent business support publications. The first is the *Exporters Encyclopaedia* – an annual publication that provides information and advice on exporting to almost every country in the world. The second is the *Internationl Risk and Payment Review* – a monthly publication that allows companies to keep up to date on issues affecting the local trading environment.

D&B

2

Dun & Bradstreet
Austin
Texas 78731
❏ Tel: +800 234 3867 Outside US: +1 512 794 7768
Website: [www.DNB.com]
To order online: [custserv@dnb.com]

Or

Dun & Bradstreet
Holmer's Farm Way
High Wycombe
Bucks, HP12 4UL
❏ Tel: +44 1494 422000; fax: +44 1494 422260
Website: [www,dunandbrad.co.uk]

The Economist Intelligence Unit produces a range of quarterly and annual publications which provide a detailed political and economic analysis of Argentina. They offer a *Country Report*, an up-to-date monitoring information service, *Country Profile*, which combines historical data and background with current reportage, and a forecast service entitled the *Country Risk Service*.

EIU

EIU

The Economist Building
111 West 57th Street
New York, NY 10019
USA
❏ Tel: +1 212 554 0600; fax: +1 212 586 1181

Or

15 Regent Street
London, SW1Y 4LR
❏ Tel: +44 207 830 1000; fax: +44 207 830 1023
Website: [www.eui.com]; e-mail: [london@eui.com]

Banks, particularly the larger institutions that operate across the globe, are also a useful source of information. This can usually be accessed through the banks' websites.

Another useful source of market information and news/archive material is **Reuters Business Briefing** – a CD ROM or web-based information service allowing subscribers to search a vast range of information sources for material on virtually any subject matter. It is a good way of following and reproducing news as well as

2

following trends and tracking down information on individual companies.

Dow Jones Reuters Business Briefing
Reuters Limited
85 Fleet Street
London, EC4P 4AJ
❏ Tel: +44 20 7542 5043

Also worth bearing in mind are the trade associations – there is one for almost every conceivable industry. Some of these are large and active in promoting exports. They will assist their members to take part in trade fairs, can organise seminars and conferences to run concurrently with these events and may target particular countries where they believe the greatest opportunities exist for their members. Some known to be active in providing export assistance are:

British Footwear Association
❏ Tel: +44 20 7580 8687

British Contract Furnishing Association
❏ Tel: +44 1325 340072

Environmental Industries Commission
❏ Tel: +44 20 7935 1670

Telecommunications Industry Association
❏ Tel: +44 1908 645000

CDB Research

Full lists of all the associations in the UK are available from **CBD Research Ltd** in Kent, who publish a directory in hard copy or in CD-ROM format – full details at [www.glen.co.uk]. Further information is also available from Trade Partners UK.

Travel Advice

Information about flights, visas, etc. is contained in Chapter 3. This section deals with such matters as health concerns and security issues.

US State Department

The **US State Department** advice service can be found at: [www.state.gov/travel_warnings]. Their reports can sometimes seem alarmist as they are legally obliged to publish any threats to US citizens and their property of which they are aware. Also see [www.usis.egnet.net]

The most convenient source of travel advice from the UK is the **Foreign and Commonwealth Office** (FCO) travel advisory service. This can be accessed either by telephone or on-line. It provides succinct information and advice on natural disasters, health concerns, security and political issues. It is more than adequate for most business traveller's needs. Be aware though that it is aimed at a wide audience and is not geared solely towards the business visitor's requirements.

FCO

The FCO travel advisory service can be contacted on:

❑ Tel: +44 207 238 4503/4
Website: [www.fco.gov.uk/travel]

or in the UK on Ceefax on BBC2 page 470

For travel information and advice geared specifically towards the business traveller's needs, you must turn to the private sector. Here there are some good but expensive services which provide more frequently updated reports than the FCO or State Department travel notices. These services tend to be more forward-looking, commenting for instance on the likelihood of further security incidents or environment. They are also usually more frank about a country as they do not have the same political restraints as the FCO or State Department.

Keeping up to date

Publications

After you have thoroughly researched the Argentinian market and started operations in the country, it is essential to keep up-to-date with developments both in your particular sector and in the wider market.

The easiest way is to monitor the press and media for stories on Argentina. The country receives adequate coverage in the international press and most British newspapers and news organisations have correspondents based in the region. The interest editions of some newspapers and media organisations offer news e-mail services, which send stories on specified subjects to your e-mail address.

Others allow you to produce customised pages, which are updated with stories on your chosen subjects. One of the best is **CNN's** service [cnn.com].

More Specialised Information

Although you have thoroughly researched Argentina, you may still need more information, analysis and advice. You may need detailed information on prospective partners or analysis geared towards your specific project or business environment you are entering. Detailed investigation and analysis tailored to particular specifications costs money. This course is really only viable for companies involved in large projects or where there is a lot at stake.

The companies mentioned below – Control Risks, Kroll Associates and Pinkertons – all provide confidential assessments of the business environments you'll be operating in in Argentina, and provide detailed information on the people and companies with which you might form strategic partnerships.

Control Risk Group
1749 Old Meadow Road
Suite 120
McLean, VA 22102
❏ Tel: +703 893 0083; fax: +1 703 893 8611
Website: [www.crg.com]

83 Victoria Street
London
SW1H 0HW
❏ Tel: +44 207 222 1552; fax: +44 207 222 2296

Kroll Associates
900 3rd Ave
New York, N.Y. 10022-4728
❏ Tel: +1 212 593 1000; fax: +1 212 593 2631
E-mail: [info@kroll-ogara.com]

25 Savile Row
London
W1X 0AL
❏ Tel: +44 207 396 0000; fax: +44 207 969 2631
Website: [www.krollworldwide.com]

Pinkerton Corporate Offices
4330 Park Terrace Drive
Westlake Village, CA 91361
❏ Tel: +1 818 706 6800; fax: +1 818 706 5515
Website: [www.Pinkertons.com]

2

Ferrari House
102 College Road
Harrow
Middx HA1 1ES
❏ Tel: +44 20 8424 8884; fax: +44 20 8424 9744
E-mail: [jbpcisuk@aol.com]

2

The Republic of Argentina

getting there

getting there

Entry Requirements

Citizens of the United States and European Union do not require visas.

It is best to consult your nearest Argentine Consulate if you are in any doubt.

Business visas are issued through your nearest Consulate Section of the Argentine Embassy. You will need to present your passport, complete an Application Form, have a letter from your employer confirming your status with your company and the purpose of your visit or a letter of invitation if a tourist (depending on nationality). There is a fee of about US$40 or £22 and the visa will normally take two working days to be issued.

Business Visas

Health and Insurance

Most business visitors to Argentina get no further than Buenos Aires on their first visit. No particular health precautions are required. Tap water is drinkable and hygiene standards are high. Pasteurised milk and dairy products are equally safe. Locally produced meat, poultry, fish, seafood, vegetables and fruit are safe to eat but thorough washing of uncooked fruit and vegetables is recommended.

Vaccinations: No certificates of vaccination are required to enter Argentina but it is recommended that if you intend to visit some provinces then you might want to check with the Argentine authorities that there are no localised health risks. There is a small risk of malaria in the more isolated rural areas of Salta, Jujuy, Missiones and Corrientes.

Vaccinations

Hepatitis A and gastroenteritis are fairly common outside the main cities and towns but present little problem within towns and conurbations.

There are no reciprocal health agreements in force and any accident or illness requiring hospitalisation can be expensive – insurance is recommended.

Medical facilities throughout Argentina are generally good by South American standards and comparable with European countries. Argentine doctors are well trained. A consultation can cost between US$25 and US$200.

Medical Insurance

3

A 24-hour pharmacy service is available and this can be found under the heading Farmacias de Turno in your local paper. Pharmacies can sell many drugs without a prescription and also routinely administer any injections prescribed by your doctor.

What to Wear

Buenos Aires is a sophisticated cosmopolitan city where dress is more inclined towards European than North American tastes. If anything, there is a little more formality about dress in Argentina than in the rest of South America. Men are expected to wear suits or smart blazers and casual wear. Women are very fashion-conscious and take great pains over dress, make-up, coiffure and accessories. Even in the evening amongst friends, Argentines are fastidiously neat. Bermuda shorts, baggy trousers, T-shirts and sandals are all frowned on outside the beach resorts. If you need to buy clothes or shoes bear in mind that Argentina uses the European sizing system.

Climate

Most of Argentina has a temperate climate except for the north-east, which is hot and humid, and the mountainous west, which has a greater variation between hot and cold. If you go to Patagonia be prepared for some seriously cold and inhospitable weather!

Buenos Aires has seasons which are the reverse of the northern hemisphere.

The summer months are January and February, when the suffocating heat and high humidity drive locals to seek the cool breezes of Mar del Plata or Punta del Este on the Atlantic seaboard. Temperatures from December onwards are 20°C+, but temperatures of 30°C and more are frequent and 40°C is not unknown. These months are not good times to do business in Buenos Aires since millions, including most of the decision makers, leave the city on holiday. Office hours are reduced but business is still conducted in a formal setting of collar and tie for men and smart summer outfits for women. In the high humidity, cotton and linen are recommended.

3

June, July and August are winter months. The temperature in Buenos Aires can drop to around 5°C but rarely dips below 10°C. It has not snowed in Buenos Aires since 1918! Woollen suits are usually adequate and heavy overcoats are unnecessary, though Buenos Aires ladies of fashion will get their fur coats out at the first excuse! Men usually wear light overcoats and scarves during the winter.

Rain is a possibility at any time of the year in Buenos Aires, the heaviest rainfall being in March and October. The sub-tropical north of Argentina has the heaviest rainfall and the south gets wetter and colder the closer you get to Tierra del Fuego, at which point sub-Arctic temperatures prevail. It is always wise to take a raincoat or umbrella with you on any long trip to Argentina.

Flights

Contact details for the international airline offices are listed in Appendix 1.

Buenos Aires has two airports. Intercontinental flights use **Ezeiza Airport**, but some neighbouring countries and internal flights use **Jorge Newberry Airport** (*Aeroparque*).

Ezeiza: Ezeiza is the major international airport. It is served by many major airlines including: Aerolineas Argentinas, British Airways, Iberia, Lufthansa, Air France, KLM, Swissair, Alitalia, Aeroflot, United Airlines, American Airlines, Canadian, South African Airlines, Varig, Pluna, Lan Chile, Aero Perú and Líneas Aéreas Paraguayas.

Ezeiza is located 35 kms. south of the city and is connected by a fast toll road to the centre. Transportation is available by limousine, taxi and bus. Car hire (Hertz, National, Avis) is also available but driving a car in Argentina before being thoroughly used to local driving habits and conditions can be very dangerous.

The journey will take about half an hour to the centre, up to one hour or more at peak traffic times, It is always best to allow one hour for the journey, just in case.

On leaving customs do not accept any offers from supposed taxi drivers approaching passengers in the

3

Airports

terminal. You will inevitably be ripped off! Just outside the customs hall, once you have thrust your way through the crowds of families waiting to greet passengers, you will see official transport companies who can offer you a fixed price journey into Buenos Aires. Go to these companies and buy a ticket , present it to your remise, taxi or bus driver immediately outside the terminal doors. You must buy a ticket inside the terminal to use the service and payment to the drivers is not allowed.

Private-hire limousines, will take you straight to your hotel. The fare will be around US$45. These are comfortable and safe, but the drivers do not always speak English. A dollar or two tip is enough.

Taxis

An ordinary taxi (easily recognisable by its black body and yellow roof) will cost anything up to US$70 depending where in the city you want to go. It is best to write the address down and show it to the driver since they do not usually speak English, and it is also a good idea to ask him exactly what it will cost before you let him put the luggage in his cab! All cabs should display a notice inside, usually hung down the back of the driver's seat, showing their licence and the driver's details. If the cab does not have one of these, do not get in. Make sure the cab has a meter which is switched on when you begin your journey and that the rates for luggage, waiting time etc. are clearly displayed. A dollar or two tip is sufficient.

Minibus

The cheapest option is a fast and frequent coach and minibus service run by Manuel Tienda León. These take you to the very centre of town, from where there are a plentiful supply of taxis to take you on cheaply to your hotel or final destination in the city. Cost: US$15 each way. The buses arrive and depart at approximately half-hour intervals from 0500 until 2300.

There is also a coach service from Ezeiza to Aeroparque airport. There is no metro or train link to Ezeiza.

There is a departure tax of US$13 for leaving Ezeiza payable in pesos or dollars. You cannot pay with a credit card so keep back enough cash for your return journey. Duty Free is available but the range of goods is limited.

Jorge Newberry (Aeroparque)

This airport is usually known as **Aeroparque** and is located in the northern suburbs beside the river, only ten to fifteen minutes from downtown by taxi. It is used mainly for domestic flights and flights to Montevideo. Airlines operating from Aeroparque include Aerolineas Argentinas, Austral and LADE. There are no connecting flights for the short distance to Ezeiza International Airport.

Aeroparque is served by ordinary taxis and buses. There is no metro or rail link. Again, always check that you use an official yellow-and-black taxi cab from the ranks outside the Arrivals Terminal and ask how much the fare will be before you get in the cab. These cabs are metered so make sure the driver uses it!

There is a Departure Tax for all flights out of Aeroparque (currently US$5) which is collected in pesos or dollars.

Departure Tax

By Land

Argentina has many border crossings and usually there is a bus service connecting the nearest towns on both sides of the border.

There are rail links to Bolivia and Paraguay (irregular and unreliable), but none to Brazil, Chile or Uruguay.

If you enter by car do not forget you need an International Driver's licence and appropriate documentation proving ownership and insurance.

By Sea

There is a daily ferry service across the Rio de la Plata between Montevideo (Uruguay) and Buenos Aires and another service upriver from Colonia.

3

4

after arrival

after arrival

4

...getting familiar with the way of life.

Currency

Since the Argentine peso is pegged to the dollar on a one-to one basis conversion is relatively easy. Banks and foreign exchange houses (*Casas de Cambio*) are plentiful in all major cities. Dollars are usually accepted as easily as pesos for cash transactions and credit card facilities are widely available. It is best to take a good amount of cash with you, in dollars, since commissions for changing travellers cheques can be high and some shops will surcharge you for the use of your credit card.

The *Casa de Cambio* or bank will display current exchange rates and commission charges in the window and since this is a very competative business there is little point in shopping around for marginally better rates. *Casas de Cambio* stay open into the evening but banking hours are weekdays from 1000 to 1500. The major credit cards are widely accepted, and ATMs are to be easily found around the cities.

Casas de Cambio

Getting Around

4

Distances			

Outside Buenos Aires most business trips are undertaken by air since distances are considerable, rail uncomfortable and slow, and road journeys can be lengthy and dangerous! Here are some comparative journey times from Buenos Aires:

	ROAD	AIR	RAIL
Córdoba	9 hrs	1 hr 10 mins	12 hrs
Mendoza	17 hrs	1 hr 50 mins	30 hrs
Mar del Plata	4 hrs	40 mins	4 hrs
Rosario	4 hrs	50 mins	4 hrs

Driving

Driving in Argentina is on the right and is considered even by most Argentines as far from safe, especially outside the major cities. The death rate on the roads is relatively high by North American and European standards. If you have to use a car you will need an International Driver Permit from your own country and it must be authenticated and stamped in the offices of the Automóvil Club de Argentina in Buenos Aires on Avenida Libertador 1850 ❏ tel: 802 6061/7061.

Rail

Argentina has one of the world's most extensive railway networks but by no means the most comfortable or efficient. There are over 40,000 kilometres of track but much of it is in poor state of repair and journey times are very slow (*see* chart, page 65). Many services, particularly in outlying areas, have been withdrawn. Long distance trains offer first class accommodation with sleeping and dining facilities but the journey is likely to be subject to delays and will be far from a smooth ride on many routes. The train services are run by Ferrocarriles Argentinos and tickets can be purchased either at their downtown office in Buenos Aires (Maipu 88, ❏ tel:331 3280) or at the railway station of departure.

Buenos Aires has three main railway stations:

Retiro Station downtown serves Rosario, Mendoza, Córdoba and Tucumán to the north-west. It is also the central station for the extensive local railway services into the wealthy northern suburbs.

Lacroze Station serves destinations to the north-east of Buenos Aires

Constitución Station serves destinations south of the city, Patagonia and the southern suburbs.

Buses

Many Argentines will tell you that long distance buses offer a better and more efficient service to the provinces than the railways. Some operate services to Brazil, Chile, Paraguay and Uruguay and most can be booked through travel agents in the city. Neither buses nor trains are particularly comfortable or reliable, however, so take the plane whenever you can!

Within Buenos Aires there are excellent and frequent bus services criss-crossing the city. They are known as *colectivos* and are frequently crowded during peak travel times. *Colectivos* are very cheap and frequent but their drivers are famously individualistic in their approach to

4

their work, so a ride can be pretty jerky as they swerve in and out of traffic or screech to a halt to pick up and drop off passengers. Worth a ride just for the experience!

The Metro (Subte)

Buenos Aires has an excellent underground metro system known as the Subte (short for Subterranean) which has served the city since 1913 (*see* page 116). Most of the five main lines have an excellent frequency of service with more than five minutes between trains being unusual during weekdays. This is by far the quickest and cheapest way to get around the city, but the service is designed to serve the west and north of the city only and to connect the Retiro and Constitución railway stations. It is also safe, clean and fast with trains running from 5.30 a.m. to 1.30 the following morning except at weekends when there is a reduced service. Payment is at a flat rate with tokens, known as *fichas*, which are available from kiosks and the Subte stations. The south of the city is not served at all.

Taxis

Taxis are plentiful in Buenos Aires (except when it rains!) and can be hailed in the street or found at the many taxi ranks dotted throughout the city centre and main suburbs. Most taxi drivers are honest and efficient but few speak good English. Taxis are metered and you should check that the meter is at zero before the journey begins. Tip lightly; change to the nearest peso or an extra peso for a longer journey is quite enough.

It is also worth ensuring that you know exactly the value of any banknotes you hand to the driver since taxi drivers have been known to switch banknotes or claim the amount tendered was incorrect, though this is unusual.

Communications

Argentina has not been the best country in the world for telecommunications though it has improved immensely in the last five years. Many numbers have changed or are changing so do not rely on the directories too much. As a general rule it is worth using your hotel phone as much as possible to arrange business meetings etc. Though this may involve a surcharge, it is money well spent to avoid the frustration of battling the telephone system on your own!

4

Public telephones

If you need to use a public payphone (either a yellow-and-green plastic cabin in the street or an orange one in bars and cafés) you will first need to buy a token (*ficha*) from a newspaper kiosk in the street or the barman in the bar or café. Since each token will only last you about two minutes at the most, depending on the time of day, it is best to buy a few at a time.

Long-distance calls

Long-distance calls are still expensive. These can be dialled from your room or by the hotel operator but they are usually heavily surcharged. Check the rate per minute before using the international lines if you do not want a shock when you come to check out! A cheaper way is to visit the ENCOTEL offices dotted throughout the city, where you can use a cabin to book a cheaper rate international call to Europe and the USA. The ENCOTEL office on Avenida Corrientes 707 in downtown Buenos Aires offers a 24-hour service for calls, telegrams and faxes.

4

It is still not unknown for telephones to be knocked out temporarily for whole districts when the rains persist or the city suffers a *tormenta*, the torrential sub-tropical storms that deposit inches of rain in only a few minutes. If you get caught in one, just go into a café and have a quiet drink until it is over, if you do not want to get soaked trying to get a cab before the natives get to it first! Manners tend to go out of the window during a storm and it is every man for himself! *Tormentas* do not usually last long and when they occur everyone knows appointments will be missed.

Mobile phones are widely used and the France Telecom/Telefonica partnership has set up a solid international communications structure that means that visitors' phones will function normally on the network.

Post

Postal services are reliable but slow. The main Post Office is on Sarmiento 189 and is open on weekdays until 1900. Usually your hotel will have stamps for sale and will post all mail for you.

Media

Argentina has five television stations and innumerable radio stations. American and British radio stations can be received. Most hotels have cable television offering

American and British imports and some Brazilian soap operas as well as other national and international programmes. Many are dubbed in Spanish. Sport is well represented and CNN is almost always available.

The national newspapers regarded as most important are: *La Nación, Clarín* and *Página 12*. Business news is presented more fully in Ambito Financiero.

Newspapers

Buenos Aires has an excellent daily newspaper in English called the *Buenos Aires Herald* which gives short summaries of the main political, social and economic developments of the day, full cinema and theatre listings, and all scheduled arrivals and departures for the airports and the seaport. Sport is well represented and results from British, European and North American sporting events, especially football and baseball matches, are reported, usually the same day.

All the newspapers, together with the international publications such as *Time, Newsweek, The Economist, The Financial Times, US News Report, The Miami Herald, The Times, The New York Times, La Stampa, Le Figaro, La Prensa, Die Zeitung, Panorama, Hello,* etc., are available at many kiosks throughout the city but especially on Florida and Lavalle Streets. You may have to ask for the *Buenos Aires Herald* since the demand for it is not great and some kiosks do not have it on prominent display.

Usually the latest edition of these publications is available in Buenos Aires within a few days of publication in North America or Europe. They are not so easily or widely obtained in cities outside the capital or the downtown area.

Crime

One of the interesting heritages of an authoritarian past is a deeply embedded respect for the forces of law and order. As a result, crime rates are lower than anywhere else on the continent, and violent crime is very rare. Buenos Aires is generally a very safe city.

Eating and Drinking

Argentines love food and you will soon understand why. It is no place for a vegetarian (though there are a few vegetarian restaurants) but with arguably the finest steak

4

in the world and the best Italian and Spanish cooking available outside Europe there is plenty to satisfy even the most refined tastes or the heartiest appetites.

Even modest restaurants usually serve prime meat and vegetables, carefully prepared and well served. Prices are very reasonable by European and American standards. Most dishes are washed down with the excellent local wines from Mendoza and a bottle of mineral water.

Food is offered from the highest Parisian standards down to the cheapest fast-food imaginable. At the cheaper end of the market you will find *tenedor libre* (free fork) fast-food restaurants, often Chinese, offering a fixed price all-you-can-eat menu for as little as US$5. The ingredients are not always of the best quality and often the dishes look suspiciously reheated. Many restaurants also offer fixed menus at very reasonable prices. Watch out for any extras though – they often try to squeeze more profit out of customers on mineral water and beers, etc.

4

Standard, no-frills restaurants abound and offer excellent local food based on Argentine favourites such as steak, salad, french fries, etc. Portions are generous and there is usually a large selection. Even in ordinary restaurants there will be a variety of beef cuts from which to choose and other favourites such as *Milanesa* (breaded veal). Fish will be on the menu but not with the same variety as meat dishes. Waiters do not often speak English but they will usually try and help you through the menu or find someone in the restaurant who can. In the downtown Buenos Aires restaurants the menus are normally in Spanish and English anyway.

Parrillada

A full mixture of different grilled meats is known as a *parrillada* and will often include black sausage, kidneys, various bits of intestine, etc. as well as a generous cut of beefsteak or lamb. This is accompanied by a salad of lettuce, tomato and onion to which you add olive oil and vinegar to suit your taste and perhaps a generous portion of fried or sauté potatoes. Wash this down with a good red wine (the house wines are usually very palatable) and finish it off with a nice flan or fresh strawberries and cream to feel suitably replete with simple but delicious food!

Italian food in Buenos Aires is acknowledged as being the best to be found outside Italy, principally because about one in three citizens of Buenos Aires is of Italian origin. The range is enormous. There are excellent pizzerias, and it is difficult to find a reasonably priced Italian restaurant which will not serve you excellent food.

Meat Lovers

A great feature of Argentine cuisine is the *parrilla*. Not to be missed by all devout carnivores! Basically this consists of meat grilled on an open fire. The origins of this course hark back to the *gaucho* cowboy food being prepared simply at the campfire on the pampas at the end of a hard day's riding. The meat will usually be beef but it also includes lamb, kid, chicken, sausages and offal in various forms. Portions are always more than generous!

What you will not find is a large variety of other ethnic restaurants in Argentina. There are ubiquitous Chinese restaurants serving much the same versions of Chinese food that you would find in New York or London, but apart from that there are very few Indian, Greek, Japanese or any other specialist eating places. Spanish food is very widely available and preferable if you prefer fish or seafood dishes.

4

Eating Habits

Unlike the English, the Argentines eat little or no breakfast. Outside the home, breakfast in a café will be no more than tea or coffee accompanied by buttered toast with marmalade or jam and perhaps a glass of fresh orange juice. Try the *medialunas* (half moon) small croissants with your tea or coffee; they come either glazed or plain and are delicious. Dunking them in your *café con leche* (milky coffee) is regarded as acceptable except in the politest of society. Breakfasts of this sort are often taken more as a mid-morning break. If you are still peckish try an *empanada* – a small type of Cornish-pasty, which contains either minced meat, cheese, hard-boiled eggs, ham, chicken or a combination of any or all of these ingredients with vegetables. Served hot or cold they are delicious.

Breakfast

Lunch is the first serious meal of the day for Argentines. Since breakfast is so light, lunch is eaten relatively early – anytime from noon onwards. It is far from a light meal and will consist usually of meat of some description, salad and potatoes followed by a fresh fruit dessert or custard flan.

You will not be surprised to learn that with the long Italian tradition in Argentine food there is a wide choice of superb ice-creams. Argentina does not, however, have a great variety of cheeses, though a good local Roquefort is available. A Spanish style Manchego cheese is commonest and is offered in various stages of maturity, or in oil, or accompanied by a quince preserve known as *membrillo*. Even if cheese is not on the menu the restaurant will usually serve it if you ask for it.

Since Argentines appreciate their food and are very sociable when eating, lunch can easily take a couple of hours. The meal is often rounded off with a small, thick coffee. Smoking is permitted in most restaurants and does not attract the social opprobrium currently found in many American and European restaurants.

Dinner is eaten late; 9 o'clock is normal or even later. Many restaurants will not serve you much before 8.30 p.m. at the very earliest. It is not unusual at all to sit down to dinner at 10 p.m. or 11 p.m. Perhaps this is designed to give time for a typical lunch to have been properly digested but more likely it is because many Argentines work until 7 or 8 p.m. and arrive home much later than Londoners or New Yorkers.

The evening meals are similar to the range offered for lunch and are characterised only by being often lengthier than their lunch time counterparts. An aperitif is normal and an after dinner brandy or liqueur is also usual.

Hotels

The classification by stars in Argentina is deceptive. Many hotels with four stars would be considered old-fashioned or badly maintained by American or European standards.

Prices vary considerably within each quality range. It is always worth asking for a special rate, especially if you intend to stay over more than a few days or over a weekend. There are often discounts for cash or if you do not require a VAT receipt.

Most hotel rooms have a television and radio but often the equipment is old and the reception poor. Hotels in the larger cities, particularly Buenos Aires, may have badly lit rooms, face noisy streets and have very old and rackety air-conditioning. Interior rooms are quieter but often smaller and dingy.

It is highly recommended that you see a room before you sign in, otherwise you may be given one of the less attractive rooms. While you are there, check the lighting, air-conditioning and street noise. Bear in mind that the traffic din will continue almost all night in the busy city centre and cranks up to quite a decibel count from early in the morning.

Eating in a hotel is usually more expensive than eating out and far less exciting.

Dry cleaning is always available, very quick and reasonably priced.

Always have your valuables, money and important documents lodged in the hotel safe.

Note: IVA (VAT) tax is 21 per cent so check it in any rates you are offered!

4

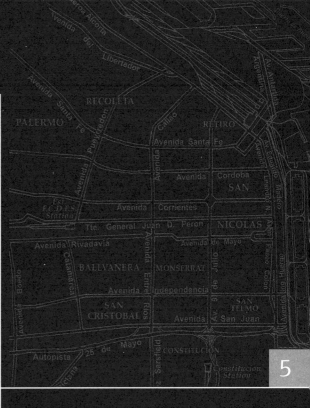

5

getting down to business

getting down to business

This chapter provides elementary guidance on the etiquette of conducting business in Argentina, and also contains details of useful local organisations who can assist with the more complicated requirements of business transactions.

Economic Overview

The biggest change in recent years affecting the
Argentine economy and business outlook is membership
of Mercosur. Argentina is now an important segment of
a huge trading block which encompasses Brazil, Chile,
Uruguay, Paraguay and Bolivia. A company now
registered in Argentina has, in effect, access to the whole
of this trading area with very few restrictions for the
movement of goods and services.

Mercosur

Apart from Mercosur Argentina operates within the
international frameworks provided by the International
Monetary Fund, The International Bank for
Reconstruction and Development, The Inter-American
Development Bank and the Latin American Integration
Association (ALADI), The World Trade Organisation
and the International Chambers of Commerce. In fact
Argentina subscribes to most of the international
organisations which regulate trade tariffs and business
property rights.

A key part of the political and economic policies of the
Menem government was the scrapping of obsolete and
restrictive practices in Argentine industry and
commercial law. Privatisation has been encouraged at a
frantic, some might say reckless pace. The old monolithic
government-controlled enterprises which were the
dominant feature of the Argentine economy during the
Peronist and military governments have almost entirely
disappeared. Foreign investment is now possible in
almost any sector of Argentine business. This has led to
very impressive short-term economic growth but there
are still problems of government expenditure and debt to
be faced.

5

Privatisation

The problem of providing services such as education,
health and efficient transport remains and many
Argentines would argue that the economic benefits of the
last Menem years have not filtered down to the general
populace. To balance the books the government is
attempting to simplify and streamline the revenue
collection system which, coupled with growing
unemployment and salary cuts for government employees,
has led to some disillusionment.

The collapse of the Brazilian currency in 1995 led to an
economic crisis in Argentina which in turn led to a credit

squeeze that forced many companies, particularly the small and medium sized ones, into bankruptcy. GDP fell and unemployment rose. Argentina is only now recovering the growth rates enjoyed before the crash but unemployment continues to rise – at one point reaching 18 per cent.

Part of the unemployment problem is the increase in the working population, mainly women entering the workforce for the first time. Another contributory factor is the high cost of labour in Argentina relative to the biggest competitor in Mercosur, Brazil. The national minimum wage of US$200 a month is no indicator of real incomes. Workers in agriculture remain by far the lowest paid. Workers in manufacturing can expect to earn around US$900 a month and those in the financial sector can expect around double that. On top of salaries, a company must pay an additional 32 per cent to the government as contributions to pensions, social security costs, etc. Employing an Argentine worker is expensive for the employer, and dismissing them can also be costly. Severance packages are based on length of service and are modelled on the European social security system.

Although one in ten Argentines still work in the agricultural sector, the numbers in industry have declined to around one in four workers. The rest are in services. Skilled workers can be hard to find outside Buenos Aires, especially in the new technologies. Working hours are long, normally well over 40 hours a week and often including Saturday. It is still not uncommon for Argentines to have more than one job even with such long hours. Many make up extra income from taxi driving, giving private lessons, or running their own small business from home.

Patents and Trade Marks

Before considering exporting to Argentina it is strongly advised that you patent your product and register your Trade Marks in Argentina. This can be done in your home country or in Argentina but it is an essential step not only to protect your company but also to use as a reference for all agreements with other companies in Argentina. That said, infringement of intellectual copyright is not a major issue in Argentina.

Import/Export

Mercosur

On 1 January 1995 the Mercosur economic trading bloc came into being. This is a free trading area, similar to NAFTA or the European Union and is formed by Argentina Brazil, Paraguay and Uruguay with Bolivia and Chile as associate members. The large market has enabled Argentina and Brazil in particular to facilitate the freer movement of goods and services throughout the region by abolishing tariff barriers on almost all products traded within the bloc. There is also a common tariff barrier between Mercosur and the rest of the world with a sliding scale of taxes on all imported goods in to Mercosur ranging from 0 to 20 per cent and, in exceptional circumstances beyond 20 per cent.

Since 1988 Argentina has operated a pre-shipment inspection scheme for all orders valued at over US$800. This will be paid for by a 1 per cent tax on the goods.

Customs duties are levied on a sliding scale of CIF value for all goods entering the country. The classification system is the Harmonised System (HS) used in most countries. A copy of the classification of products under this system should be available through your own national Ministry of Commerce, Trade Ministry or customs authorities.

5

Customs duties

Certain restrictions apply to imported foodstuffs, pharmaceuticals and products containing cattle by-products but most other goods can enter freely or can be admitted under special import licences. If in doubt, consult your nearest Commercial Attachés office in the Argentine Embassy.

The key factor to bear in mind when assessing import costs is the point of origin of the goods. Mercosur goods (*see* above) have different tariffs to goods from outside the Mercosur.

Goods from outside Mercosur attract a statistical tax of 0.5 per cent of CIF value if they are raw materials or consumer goods in finished or part-finished form but not if they are capital goods or IT telecommunication equipment. This will change in 2001 as a tariff of 14 per cent will apply to capital IT and telecommunications imported into Mercosur, rising to 16 per cent by 2006.

Textiles, footwear and clothing are sensitive areas for importers and are governed by specific regulations concerning nominal values of goods, specific labelling requirements and certification of origin.

The importation of all automobiles is strictly controlled and subject to specific legislation and quotas.

Importation of firearms, weaponry or security equipment of any kind is tightly controlled, and there are increasing restrictions on the import of chemicals, chemical products and chemical waste materials in particular.

Importers also pay 21 per cent VAT, which is also the rate applied to locally manufactured goods. The government requires 9 per cent of the VAT to be paid in advance and there is a 3 per cent withholding tax on anticipated profits. These are treated as tax credits when the annual VAT return is calculated.

5

Apart from those products and areas of commercial activity mentioned above, Argentina is remarkably free from protectionist import policies, regulations and tariffs (*see* contact details for the Chamber of Commerce in Appendix 1). Nevertheless it is essential to verify the regulations in force up to the very day of shipment before attempting to export any goods to Argentina.

Argentine customs are strict on documentation. All paperwork should be in Spanish and presented in the original form with three duplicates.

Exportation

Just as importation has recently been freed of over-regulation so exportation has become much easier in the last decade. Almost all quotas and tariffs have been abolished along with annoying red tape and fees for official paperwork and services. Consult the Ministry of Industry and Commerce in Buenos Aires if you have any doubts.

You will have to register as an exporter but, apart from giving you access to a few government export incentives and tax breaks, this is mainly to facilitate the collection of statistical information by the government.

There are some incentives for exporters including credit lines through the Central Bank, **Banco de la Nación**

Argentina (BNA), particularly for the agricultural sector, but most incentives are based on taxation benefits for the exporter, though there have been some initiatives to make insurance for exporters also more easily and cheaply available. There are some credit schemes available but many do not apply for trade within Mercosur.

VAT on exported goods is refundable, as are all import duties and taxes for goods which are imported, processed and then re-exported. Since this is calculated on the export FOB value there is in effect a taxation reduction for the company.

Pre-clearance for exportation is not usually required but you may need certification from the Ministry of Agriculture or Health that certain goods, livestock or pharmaceutical products conform to industry standards of quality and production. These regulations change fairly regularly. The best route is to consult the Argentine Commercial Office in your country or to appoint a *Despachante* in Buenos Aires familiar with your trading sector. They will also fill in all necessary customs forms which are compulsory for statistical information gathering purposes and to justify any exportation benefits.

It is worth insuring your goods and this must be done through an Argentine insurer if you wish to work with any government incentive schemes or to reclaim tax. Most goods are not inspected on export unless they are sensitive items such as arms, explosives, etc.

All goods require a commercial invoice in Spanish. It must conform to Argentina regulations. It is also advisable to provide a Packing List and, in some cases, a certificate of origin supplied by the Argentine Government. Also check that any necessary health or sanitary certificates are supplied. The bill of lading should be as detailed as possible.

Contact
Secretariat of Industry, Commerce & Mining
Secretaría de Industria, Comercio y Minería
Av. Julio A. Roca 657
1322 Buenos Aires
❏ Tel: +54 1 349 3000 or 349 3407/8; fax: +54 1 349 3477

Export incentives

VAT

5

Insurance

Chamber of Argentine Importers
Cámara de Importadores de la República Argentina
Av. Belgrano 427, Piso 7
1092 Buenos Aires
❑ Tel: +54 1 342 1101 or 342 0523; fax: +54 1 345 3003

Chamber of Argentine Exporters
Cámara de Exportadores de la República Argentina
Av. Roque Saenz Peña 740, Piso 1
1035 Buenos Aires
❑ Tel: +54 1 328 9583 or 394 4482; fax: +54 1 328 9583

Argentine Chamber of Commerce
Cámara Argentina de Comercio
Av. Leandro Alem 36, Piso 8
1003 Buenos Aires
❑ Tel: +54 1 331 8051/5 or 343 9423; fax: +54 1 331 8055

Secretariat for Agriculture, Livestock, Fishing and Food
Secretaría de Agricultura, Ganadería, Pesca y
Alimentación
Av. Paseo Colón
1063 Buenos Aires
❑ Tel : +54 1 349 2500/08; fax: +54 1 349 2504

5

Chamber of Commerce, Industry and Production
Cámara de Comercio, Industria y Producción de la
República Argentina
Calle Florida 36, Piso 4
1005 Buenos Aires
❑ Tel: +54 1 342 8252 or 331 0813; fax: +54 1 331 9116

Argentine Central Bank
Banco Central de la República Argentina (BCRA)
Reconquista 266
1003 Buenos Aires
❑ Tel: +54 1 394 8411/8119; fax: +54 1 334 6489/6468

Foreign Trade and Investment Bank
Banco de Inversión y Comercio Exterior (BICE)
Av. 25 de Mayo 526
1002 Buenos Aires
❑ Tel: +54 1 313 9546; fax: +54 1 311 5596

National Customs Administration
Administración Nacional de Aduanas
Azopardo 350
1328 Buenos Aires
❑ Tel: +54 1 343 0661/9; fax: +54 1 331 9881 or 345 1778

National Service for Agricultural Sanitation and Quality
Servicio Nacional de Sanidad y Calidad Agroalimentaria
(SENASA)
Av. Paseo Colón 367
1063 Buenos Aires
❏ Tel: +54 1 342 3231/1029; fax: +54 1 331 3843

Payment/Protection and Taxation

It is normal in Argentina to operate on the basis of a
Letter of Credit or bank draft. Some local companies
may not be happy about the expense involved but it is
strongly recommended that you insist on some such
security at least for the first transaction or two. It is also
not unusual at the beginning of a business relationship to
request part or full prepayment.

Letters of Credit

Argentina has been covered by the Investment Promotion
and Protection Agreement since 1990 and the Double
Taxation Agreement with the United Kingdom since 1996.

Since the peso and the US dollar are at a parity much
quoting of prices and invoicing is done in dollars, even if
the country of origin is not the United States. Some
sterling, French francs, Italian lire and Deutschmark
invoicing is also normal, but the Euro has not established
itself yet and other currencies from outside Mercosur and
Chile are not commonly used.

5

Business Etiquette

Argentine business people are more European than
American in their approach to business. Appearance is
considered important. Business men and women are
almost always well dressed and groomed. Suits are
recommended for men, and conservative dress for
women. Even at the height of a humid Buenos Aires
summer, men normally wear long sleeved shirts and a
tie and a light weight suit or smart blazer.

As befit the Mediterranean origins of Argentine culture it
is normal to offer a generous handshake on first
acquaintance and if you are present when Argentines
greet each other do not be surprised to see the men give
each other a quick embrace and pat on the back or the
women a quick peck on the cheek.

Greetings

You will be expected to offer a business card on first
acquaintance.

Appointments

When making appointments bear in mind that it is often as easy to get an appointment with key executives at the end of the day as it is first thing in the morning. Many arrive late and leave late. Office hours vary in the summer but are normally 0900 to 1900 except for government offices. It is always best to be on time for appointments even if you are kept waiting. Argentines try to be punctual themselves and admire punctuality in others. If you are going to be late it is courteous to phone and let them know.

Speaking Spanish

Most Argentine business people in the cities, especially Buenos Aires, have a reasonable command of English but this is not always the case in the smaller cities and towns. It is always appreciated if you make at least some attempt to greet them and introduce yourself in Spanish. Fluency in Spanish is not expected and Argentines are tolerant of mistakes since your courtesy in trying to speak their language is more important than accuracy. You can, of course, hire interpreters but they are usually expensive.

5

If you are from the United States, it is best to introduce yourself as a North American since the term 'American' in Argentina can mean anyone from North, Central or South America and it may sound arrogant for United States citizens to claim the title exclusively for themselves.

Negotiations are usually begun with the offer of coffee or some other beverage. It is polite to accept. There is likely to be a considerable amount of polite small talk before getting down to business. This is important and should not be rushed. Always allow longer for meetings in Argentina than you would at home.

Argentines like to feel they know something of the person with whom they will do business as well as the business itself. They do not appreciate too direct or blunt an approach to business considerations at the start of a meeting. Establishing a good working relationship with you and your team is more important than the status of your company at this stage. Many Argentines view international business as a personal matter between individuals.

Although not as demonstrative as some other Latin Americans, the Argentines can be heated on key points in business and will be aggressive in defending their own professional reputation. It is courteous in Argentine society and South American culture in general to help you and your business in any way.

If you are doing business in the provinces it is not wise to sing the praises of Buenos Aires. The old rivalry which caused so much unrest and jealousy in the last century still exists in some parts. The provinces often feel that Buenos Aires, though home to one third of the population, has a disproportionate amount of wealth and power. The *Porteños*, as residents of Buenos Aires are called, are sometimes thought arrogant and patronising towards their supposedly less sophisticated country cousins. Citizens of Mendoza and Córdoba. both of which have deeper cultural roots than Buenos Aires, appreciate visitors who recognise their proud colonial and post-colonial heritage.

Since Argentines hold strong opinions on political, social and sporting matters it is easy for a discussion to degenerate into an argument. Some Argentines tend to make a definitive statement and then defend it to the last. Changing one's mind is perhaps taken as a sign of weakness rather than open-mindedness. The raised voices and animated gestures of Argentines debating amongst themselves can be disconcerting to the newcomer, but accept that much of this is bluster.

Always try to meet the person as high up the totem pole as you can. There is still a strong centralised 'boss' culture in many Argentine companies in which, no matter how enthusiastic others may be about your proposition, the final word rests with the man at the top. Much time can be wasted on negotiations which founder because you have failed to influence the real decision makers. Try and find out exactly who you are dealing with within a company and who they answer to for key decisions.

Choice of venue is another important aspect of business meetings. Suggesting a first meeting in an informal atmosphere, such as a hotel or other neutral setting, is always appreciated. Remember that formality is appreciated and you will be judged on your personality and appearance as much as your product. It is quite possible that the first person you meet may simply be assessing you for the ultimate decision maker in their company.

5

Meeting the decision makers

When meeting a team of Argentine negotiators it is essential to identify who's who in the team. Usually there will be one principal negotiator who will do most of the talking and expect you to do most of the talking to him or her. The rest of the team may contribute little to the discussion and are there to supply professional expertise. Even if you find a talkative member of the team do not think progress can be made by convincing him of your case. Do not be confrontational especially with the lead negotiator. Loss of face on his or her part will be deeply resented and you are likely to fail. No matter how heated the discussion, stay calm and avoid personalising the argument. Always have a fall-back position, and it is often wise to suggest a short break for coffee or tea to take the heat out of the atmosphere.

Remember, this can be a much longer process than you are used to at home, and Argentines resent being rushed. It is acceptable and proof of seriousness to make notes during the meeting and punctuate your responses with periods of thoughtful silence. As with anyone else, Argentines should be taken very seriously indeed. Try and anticipate what their position is likely to be, and why, so that you have alternatives ready to propose. Back this up whenever possible with statistics.

Argentine business people may be prone occasionally to offer more than they can deliver. This is not ill-meant, it is a genuine desire to be as helpful and positive as possible.

Finally, do not be afraid to terminate negotiations if you feel there is no point in continuing, but do not threaten to do so unless you really mean it, and be careful how you do it. Remember that personal impressions are crucial and the networking in the Argentine business community will ensure that your reputation will go before you into any subsequent negotiations. Maintain your reputation for professionalism and politeness. Being tough but fair is acceptable, aggression and rudeness are not.

Entertaining

If you are unsure where to entertain your Argentine guest for lunch, ask his secretary to book you a table. Most Argentines take eating seriously and regard it principally as a social rather than business event. It is another opportunity for them to get to know you better. Keep business conversation light during the meal and save any serious considerations until after the dessert.

Public Holidays	
January 1	Bank Holiday
Good Friday	Easter
May 1	Labour Day
May 26	Anniversary of First Republican Government
June 20	Day of the National Flag
July 9	National Day
August 17	Anniversary of the death of General San Martín
October 12	Columbus Day
December 25	Christmas Day

Note. It is not unknown for people to take longer breaks around these public holidays. These are known as *puentes* (bridges) and it may be difficult to find everyone in their offices during these periods.

5

It is not customary to drink at lunchtime, except for wine with a meal. It is acceptable to invite colleagues of the same gender to have a drink near the office or at your hotel but this may be declined for family reasons. Remember it is a long business day usually running from 0900 to 1800 and that many executives regularly stay at work well after office hours.

The evening meal is unlikely to take place much before 2100 and can often go on until midnight or beyond. Wine is usually drunk and it would be a compliment to ask your Argentine guest to choose a fine Argentine wine to accompany the meal. If you are paying, check that the menu includes VAT (21 per cent) and leave a tip of no more than 10 per cent – many Argentines will tell you even that is far too much and will be horrified at your naïve generosity if you leave more. Credit cards are widely accepted, especially Visa, Mastercard, American Express and Diners Club.

You may well be invited to the home of your Argentine colleagues, but always check if it is to be a formal dinner invitation or an informal gathering. It is customary to take a small gift – chocolates, flowers or wine – for the hostess, but do not be too punctual for invitations of this sort – it is best to be at least fifteen minutes late.

5

6

industry overviews

industry overviews

6

Foreign Investment

Approximately 40 per cent of foreign investment in Argentina comes from the USA, and the percentage is growing. Of the rest, another third comes from the European Union, and the reminder largely from Brazil, Chile and Asia. Protectionism is dead and the take-over of ailing companies by foreign investors is now actively encouraged by the government.

The traditional importance of agriculture and agricultural products to the economy has been largely replaced over the last five years by the growing significance of the service sector. Although agriculture still accounts for some 7.3 per cent of the economy, service industries now account for almost 60 per cent. The balance is made up from the industry and manufacturing sectors, which have been in decline since the free market policies of Mercosur has opened the door to increased competition.

The financial markets equally have been opened to foreign investment for the first time. Portfolio investments in securities is now commonplace. Funds and profits can be repatriated easily, freely and immediately. Any currency can be bought openly at the current exchange rate.

6

Since virtually all sectors of the economy are open, including defence, there are many opportunities. Only one or two sectors, notably uranium mining and the nuclear power industry, remain off-limits. Investment can take almost any form - the use of assets, capital equipment, intangible assets, etc - for the pursuit of trade in Argentina. One note of warning: financing investment through credit obtained in Argentina is extremely expensive. Although lower in recent years as inflation has been squeezed out of the economy, it is best by far to fund investment internally through your company or from sources outside the country.

The Government does not discriminate against foreign companies in terms of access to government subsidies and tax incentives, but there is little available in terms of central government subsidies. Some incentives remain, usually in the form of local tax relief, available from provincial governments, especially in the fields of agriculture, mining and tourism.

Most of the foreign investment in recent years has flowed into sectors which have been privatised. The greatest beneficiaries have been the telecommunications, water, oil, gas, sewerage, mining and transportation sectors. Construction, automobiles, agricultural processing and tourism also present significant opportunities under development. Manufacture of electro-domestic goods is also renewing itself as an active part of the economy. The financial and business service sectors are also growing but the main investment has so far been in the basic infrastructural and prime material and energy production sectors.

International Trade

Almost a quarter of all Argentine trade is with Brazil. The United States accounts for some 15 per cent and the balance of trade is with the European Union, Chile, Uruguay and Japan. Together, these trading partners account for almost three-quarters of all international trade.

Exports

Exports are led by fuels, cereals, food-by-products, fats and oils, transportation equipment, metals, chemicals, oilseed, machinery and electrical equipment, leather and skin products, These sectors combined account for two-thirds of the value of all exports.

Imports

Imports have grown significantly since the scrapping of protective tariffs and barriers in the 1990s. The most significant sectors are machinery and mechanical equipment, chemicals, transportation equipment, electrical equipment, plastic and rubber products, metals, mineral product, paper and paper products, food by-products and textiles. Together these represent 70 per cent of all imports and of that, some 20 per cent is machinery and mechanical equipment. One-fifth of imports are direct consumer goods, the rest either capital equipment, and part-manufactured items for process manufacturing.

Deregulation led to a boom in foreign trade in the 1990s, which grew from under $12 billion in 1986 to $47 billion in 1996. This represented an increase of 4.5 per cent of GDP during the same period. It may look good, but it means that over 80 per cent of economic activity in Argentina is still dedicated to serving the internal Argentine market rather than foreign trade. Considering

6

that the United Kingdom regards 45 per cent of all economic activity as foreign trade related, Argentina still has room for expansion in this area.

Exports increased between 1986 and 1996 from nearly $7 billion to $24 billion but during the same period imports increased more significantly from $5 billion to $24 billion. Since much of this was Argentine industry importing machinery for modernisation purposes, the economy is now beginning to reap the benefit. The days when the latest model of car, washing machine or television set to roll off the production line was already five years or more out of date are now, thankfully, over.

Most economic activity is directed towards serving the internal economy. The Argentine workforce is still trying to adjust to the new skills required to compete successfully in international trade and to defend local industry against increased imports. It may be difficult to recruit in any number the experienced staff with knowledge of international markets and business practice. The Argentine people are highly educated and sophisticated but may lack significant knowledge of business methodology and practices of other countries.

6

Telecommunications

The state-owned telecommunications system has had a poor reputation for service, so much so that in the 1980s cable television was reputed to have more subscribers than the unreliable phone system.

Following the 1990 privatisation, however, a shared monopoly was established with Telecom (a consortium including France Telecom and Telecom Italia) and Telephónica (controlled by Telefónica de España). Effectively the country was split geographically, Telecom taking the north and Telefónica taking the south, with Buenos Aires (the largest part of the market) split down the middle. Investment has been steadily increasing with US$4 billion confirmed to cover the first 18 months of the new century. Both companies reported a squeeze on profits in the light of increasing competition; profit forecasts remained low.

Further deregulation is planned and already other representatives of the major international communications companies are establishing a foothold in the fixed line market. Advertising campaigns have so far proved largely unsuccessful in persuading users to elect a switch on their chosen service providers, but this is unlikely to deter multinationals eager to establish a long-term presence.

Telecommunications remain a vital sector for Argentina's stock market and represent a significant part of the trading which takes place. The Financial Times ranked Telecom the tenth largest company in Latin America for the financial year to September 1998, with a value of US$6.55 billion, and full year after tax profits of US$374 million.

Mobile phones

As elsewhere in the world, the mobile phone market points the way forward and continues to unsettle those companies locked uniquely into fixed line systems. Telecom Personal, the mobile phone division within Telecom, has seen a steady increase to its current rate of 1.3 million subscribers, and Telefónica is not far behind with 1.05 million users. Take-up for Internet services has also been good, although it is still below a million subscribers locally.

Agriculture

Beef

The export of beef, the lifeblood of the Argentine economy, has always been vulnerable to international demand, most noticeably during international recessions when many importers seek to become more self-sufficient.

The past ten years have seen a steady decline in the national herd, from 67 million to 50 million and the prices of the cattle on the hoof dropped by as much as a third over the same period. Exports now account for only 10 per cent of beef production, and with the growing trends for a more diverse diet, even domestic consumption has dropped.

One piece of good news has been the announcement in May 2000 by the Paris-based International Epizootic Office (IEO) that the country's cattle herd was certified free of foot-and-mouth-disease. This has, at last, opened the lucrative US market and a quota of 30,000 tons has

6

been agreed, with the hopes of further such quotas being agreed in other important export markets such as Japan, Korea, China and Mexico.

Based on hopes of re-attaining the export high of 520,000 tons of beef in 1995, the Government has embarked on a multi-million dollar campaign to re-brand Argentine beef and market it to the major international beef importing nations.

There is naturally a strong dairy industry, with sales of over $4 billion p.a. This sector has seen significant foreign investment over the last decade but is still largely dedicated to serving the domestic market rather than export.

Edible Oils and Cereals

This sector has grown dramatically and is, unlike the dairy sector, export-led. Comprising mainly soybean and sunflower seed oil, Argentine production is some four million tons a year. Argentina also produces almost four million tons of flour annually, mostly for domestic consumption, although there is significant exportation of raw grain.

Prices for Argentina's main agricultural exports have been unstable of late and farmers are finding it increasingly difficult to turn a profit. The price of wheat, maize and sunflower have all slumped over the past few years. Soya bean alone has bucked the trend, and prospects look good for increased exports in the future, dependent on weather conditions.

In line with the trend in many farming nations around the world, smaller farms are increasingly being squeezed out by the larger establishments who enjoy obvious efficiencies of scale. Over the past ten years the number of individual farms has fallen from 378,000 to 325,000 – a drop of 14 per cent – and looks set to continue to declining.

Mineral Reserves

Minerals

Argentina may have been almost a creation of the first mineral explorers, when the Spanish sailed up the estuary

6

of the River Plate in search of silver, but Argentina is only now awakening to the value of its mineral reserves.

Argentina has proven reserves of twenty valuable minerals, but in spite of this extraction has only ever at best held stable, often declining, over the past twenty years up to 1996. The overall sector contracted to its lowest point in 1991 when it was estimated at US$490 million (compared to US$870 million in 1980).

The reasons for this are largely political; the nation's infrastructure was rarely solid enough to encourage the long term investment needed. In the 1990s a more favourable regulatory framework was introduced, successfully encouraging new investment in the sector. The government promised investment of US$3.4 billion for the mining sector in the period between 1996 and 2000.

The biggest mine development remains **Bajo La Alumbrera,** a giant US$2.2 billion copper and gold mine which began production in 1997 and which is owned by MIM Holdings (50 per cent), Rio Algom (25 per cent) and North Ltd (25 per cent).

6

Oil, Gas and Petrochemicals

Argentina is the third largest Latin American oil and gas producer after Mexico and Venezuela. Crude oil output rose by almost 50 per cent in the first half of the 1990s and around two-thirds of the total is now shipped for export. Further increase in crude oil output is expected over the next few years.

Argentina's oil and gas sector has in the past been dominated by the public company, **Yacimientos Petrolíferos Fiscales** (YPF). This was privatised in 1991, however, and Repsol of Spain subsequently built on their original 15 per cent share to launch a dramatic take-over in April 1999. Speculation that the country's second biggest oil company, **Pérez Companc Group,** would be targeted by foreign buyers was, however, warded off when the Pérez Companc family strengthened control on voting rights.

Automotive fuels, diesel and other petroleum products account for almost $2.2 billion dollars of exports a year.

With abundant natural gas supplies to provide the raw material, the Petrochemical industry also flourishes, particularly around port of Bahia Blanca south of Buenos Aires, where much of the industry is concentrated.

Motor Vehicles

Argentina has manufactured motor vehicles since 1959. Initially closed to foreign competition, the market was shielded by protectionist commercial practices, with small local companies manufacturing high-cost vehicles in small, inefficient production runs, but the cost of car production in Argentina has fallen dramatically since then.

Today Argentina has a motor industry that is fairly well developed, with 11 international vehicle manufacturers as well as two local coach manufacturers, producing a wide range of vehicles. Chrysler, Fiat, General Motors and Toyota have all set up operations in Argentina and most other international manufacturers have changed their local licence agreements to secure more direct presence in the marketplace. Dina of Mexico is building a facility to manufacture trucks, ARO of Romania has announced a plant for 4 x 4 vehicles in the province of La Pampa, and Honda are reportedly researching a site for their own manufacturing facility.

During the last decade local production has risen from 100,000 units to a peak of around 500,000 in 1997, making Argentina the nineteenth largest vehicle-producing nation. This growth slowed dramatically during the 1997 recession, largely because exports to other Mercosur countries were greatly reduced. Demand from Brazil, ever the giant in the region and the economy that sets the pace for those around it, slumped suddenly, and Argentine exports fell to as little as 300,000 units. Production and sales levels are now starting to recover, and confidence in the future of the industry was also boosted by the renogotiation of the Mercosur automobile industry agreement. The previous agreement allowed for duty-free exchange of vehicles provided the number of units traded between the two nations was kept at parity – an arrangement that gave Argentine exporters access to the largest Brazilian market while still protecting their own domestic market from a flood of Brazilian imports. Fears that any new agreement would be less favourable were calmed when the new agreement, although acknowledging the imbalance, allowed for a gradual phasing-out of the

6

old arrangement, leaving the Argentine car manufacturers a period of grace to prepare for Brazil's competitive threat.

Useful Addresses

Dirección de Mercados Agrícolas y Agroindustriales
(Directorate for Administration of Agricultural and Agroindustrial Markets) Paseo Colón 922 Piso 1
1063 Buenos Aires
❏ Tel: (1) 349 2289/90

Oficina de Control Comercial Agropecuario
(National Office for the Control of Agricultural Products)
Paseo Colón 922, Piso 1
1063 Buenos Aires
❏ Tel: (1) 349 2287

Asociación de Industrias Argentinas de Carnes
(The Meat Industries Association)
San Martin 390 Piso 10
1004 Buenos Aires
❏ Tel: (1) 394 9203

Cámara Argentina de la Industria de los Oleaginosos
(Chamber of Commerce for the Agricultural Oilseed) Industry
Piedras 83
1070 Buenos Aires
❏ Tel: (1) 342 5728

Cámara Industrial de Productos Alimenticios
(Chamber of Commerce for Food Production Industry)
Av.L.N.Alem 1067 Piso 12
1001 Buenos Aires
❏ Tel: (1) 312 1929

Subsecretaría de Minería
(Government Subsecretariat for the Mining Industry)
Av. Julio A. Roca 651 Piso 2
1322 Buenos Aires
❏ Tel: (1) 349 3271/74

Subsecretaría de Industria
(Government Subsecretariat for Industry)
Av. Julio A. Roca 651
1322 Buenos Aires
❏ Tel: (1) 349 4356

6

Dirección Nacional de Combustibles
(National Directorate for the Fuel Industry)
Av. Paseo Colón 171 Piso 6
1063 Buenos Aires
❑ Tel: (1) 349 8031/2

Cámara de la Industria Petroleo
(Chamber of Commerce for the Petroleum Industry)
Av. Madero 1020 Piso 11
1106 Buenos Aires
❑ Tel: (1) 312 0410

Cámara de la Industria Química y Petroquímica
(Chemical and Petrochemical Chamber of Commerce)
Av. L.N. Alem 1067 Piso 7
1001 Buenos Aires
❑ Tel: (1) 311 7732

Comisión Nacional de Comunicaciones
(National Telecommunications Commission)
Sarmiento 151 Piso 4
1041 Buenos Aires
❑ Tel: (1) 347 9901/2

6

Asociación de Fábricas de Automotores (ADEFA)
(Automobile Manufacturers Association)
Marcelo T. Alvear 636 Piso 5
1058 Buenos Aires
❑ Tel: (1) 312 3483

7

how to set up a
permanent operation

how to set up a permanent operation

This section does not set itself up as the be-all and end-all reference for establishing an office. Its aim is to provide a sweeping overview for the visitor who is considering the possibility of a local office. The following pages highlight some of the pitfalls and benefits, give an insight into the legal situation, and run through some of the major issues to be considered, such as recruitment and finding premises.

Foreign investors are treated in the same way as domestic investors, so all options for establishing your business in whichever legal form you choose are open to you in Argentina.

All applications to form a business entity have to be approved by the **Inspección General de Justicia** (IGJ) if your business is to be based in the Federal District and by similar judicial authorities throughout the provinces. The IGJ regulates business registration and is empowered to investigate any suspected abnormalities or misdemeanours and to demand the filing of annual accounts. Outside the Federal District all documentation necessary for the formation and maintenance of a business is filed with the Commercial Registry for that province. Once established, should you wish to float your company publicly, merge with or acquire a publicly quoted company, you will be regulated by the rules of the **Comisión Nacional de Valores** (CNV). The finance and banking industries themselves are in turn regulated by the **Banco Central de la República Argentina**. Obviously, good local legal and financial advice is an essential prerequisite for deciding what kind of business to establish and where. Although much improved, many Argentine administrative procedures are lengthy and labyrinthine. They are not eased by being part of a complicated set of international, federal, provincial and local laws which occasionally require different documentation or the same documentation presented in a different way. All documentation must be in Spanish or in translations authenticated by a translator certified by the Argentine government.

Regulatory bodies

7

The following list is not definitive, but should serve as an overview of the options available and the feasibility of a particular project.

Branches

A branch in Argentina is called a *sucursal*. Many overseas companies decide that opening a branch is the easiest option. The following steps should be taken:

● A Public Notary in your own country, who has been authorised by the Argentine Embassy, must certify the authenticity of all documents.

Branches

● An application is made to the IGJ or other appropriate provincial authority for the establishment of a branch business. The application must include the articles of law governing the incorporated company in your own country, the minutes of the Board of Directors resolution to establish the branch together with the capitalisation to be allocated to the business in Argentina. There is no minimum capital investment.

● You must also provide minutes of a shareholders' meeting which nominates the Board of Directors of the branch in Argentina and there must be a Power of Attorney issued for any person who is to represent the company and corporation in Argentina.

All of this must be submitted to and published in the *Boletin Oficial*.

● You must appoint a local legal representative.

● The branch must keep separate accounts from the mother company and these must be maintained and filed in accordance with Argentine regulations.

Warning - remember that if you form a branch of your own company in Argentina which is wholly owned by your company outside Argentina then your assets inside and outside Argentina will both be at risk!

Corporations

An incorporated company in Argentina is called a *Sociedad Anónima* or SA for short. This is the preferred method of establishing a business for larger companies or those wishing to invest over the long term. This is the only type of business which is allowed to offer shares to the general public. Essentially the SA has the advantage of limited liability. Once legally incorporated, the investors are only liable personally for the amount of their investment. There need to be at least two investors, both of whom must be legally resident in Argentina, who will need to provide a minimum $12,000 between them as capitalisation, a quarter of which has to be paid in when the company is formed and the rest over the subsequent two years. There is no limit on the amount of shares a foreign investor can hold in an SA company and there are variations of shares, voting rights, stock issues, dividend preferences, capital and reduction or amplification, etc. which need careful consideration before incorporation proceeds. Although directors do not have to be shareholders they must guarantee to behave within the constitution of the company. They can serve for three years at a time and be automatically re-elected. There are some key considerations though when appointing your Board:

● The majority of the Board of Directors of an Argentine Corporation must be resident in Argentina.

● All Directors must have a legal Argentine domicile address.

● Non-residents may not be Directors.

● A quorum of the Board of Directors (at least half the members plus one) must meet and keep minutes every quarter.

● Directors' salaries and remunerations or other payment in kind must not exceed 25 per cent of the Corporation's profit in any single accounting year where the remaining three quarters is distributed as dividend.

● If no dividend is paid during any single accounting year the Directors' salaries, payments, etc. must not exceed 5 per cent of profits.

● Directors are personally liable to shareholders in the event of illegal act or activities beyond the remit of the Corporation which result in loss.

To establish a Corporation in Argentina can take two months or more. You will definitely need expert accounting and legal advice. The procedure is as follows:

● A meeting is called to identify and agree the trading purpose of the Corporation, the capital to be subscribed, the articles of incorporation agreed and the Board of Directors approved. The Articles of Incorporation must state clearly the name and legal address of the Corporation, purpose of the Corporation, capitalisation, shareholder's names and capital contribution, regulations for shareholder's meetings, rights and obligations of shareholders, regulations concerning distribution of profit and loss, and internal procedures for the running of the Corporation as appropriate and officers of the company.

Corporations

7

Corporations

● The minutes of the inaugural meeting must be carefully recorded with the deed notarised by an authorised Public Notary.

● A summary of the Notarised Articles of Incorporation must be prepared, submitted to and published in the *Boletín Oficial*.

● The resolutions, deeds and articles so approved must be submitted to the IGJ or appropriate provincial authority for inspection, authentication and registration. The Corporation does not legally exist until the company is registered and the initial 25 per cent capitalisation is paid. You can act and trade during that time but you must add the words '*en formación*'(in the process of formation) to all documentation after the name of the Corporation.

Warning - while the company is being formed you are not able to enjoy the liability limitations as director or shareholder you will be entitled to once registration is complete! If you wish to open the corporation shareholding immediately to public investment you must, in addition to the procedure outlined above, undertake the following additional steps:

● Prepare a prospectus detailing the purpose of the entity, the types of shareholding available, the proposed Articles of Incorporation, the amount of capitalisation required and at what stage, etc.

● File the prospectus with the IGJ or appropriate Provincial equivalent. This must then await approval.

● Appoint a bank to be the official representative of prospective investors. Submit to the Comisión Nacional de Valores (CNV) an application for the right to issue shares to the public. Arrange for the Bank representative and an IGJ representative to officially attend the inaugural meeting of the prospective Corporation (see above).

Limited Liability Companies

A limited liability company is known as a *Sociedad de Responsabilidad Limitada* or SRL. The main features of this kind of company is that it is formed by individual shareholders. Companies, foreign or domestic, cannot hold shares in an SRL. It is, therefore, designed for individuals, not fewer than two and not more than fifty, who must subscribe and pay the capitalisation of the company in exactly equal amounts between them. As with SAs the capitalisation must be 25 per cent paid on formation and the rest over the subsequent two years. In addition, SRL companies are governed under a different sort of regulations and taxation rules to SAs. The company itself is not taxed but rather the taxation regime pertaining to all activities of the company is assessed and paid through the taxation regime applied to the individual private shareholders. The shareholdings have to be equal in value between the partners and voting rights and responsibilities are also equally divided. A shareholder's maximum liability cannot exceed the amount paid for their shareholding in the company. Changes in share ownership have to be approved by at least 75 per cent of shareholders - worth remembering for the long term if you need a certain amount of flexibility and good will amongst your partners for the smooth running of the business! Shareholders usually have the Annual Shareholder's Meeting unless they decide to have more as stipulated in the Articles of the company. Officers of the company are appointed in a similar way to SA Corporations (*see* above) and have the same rights and responsibilities. The usual books and records must be kept and presented to the authorities.

Warning - If at any point the losses incurred by an SRL exceed the asset value of the company it is compulsory under law that it be wound up and liquidated. Failure to do so makes the shareholders personally liable for any losses incurred thereafter!

To establish a Limited Responsibility Company the following steps are necessary:

● Prepare a partnership contract between the shareholders. This becomes in effect the Articles of Incorporation governing the shareholders' rights and obligations, duties of officers, capitalisation requirements, internal company regulations and procedures for further investment, liquidation, dispute resolution, etc.

● Although not strictly necessary, it is wise and usual to have the partnership contract drawn up into a deed by a Notary Public.

● The Company deed must be submitted to and published in the *Boletín Oficial*.

● The deed is then submitted to, inspected and registered by the IGJ or appropriate provincial authority. Remember, you have no liability limitation while this process is underway and, as with Corporations, you can trade during that time. The process can take around two months or more to complete.

Joint Ventures

There are two types of legal framework for joint ventures in Argentina. One is called *Agrupaciones de Colaboración* and the other *Uniones Transitorias*. The essential difference between the two is that the former envisages an ongoing business partnership over a long term while the latter is commonly used to present a joint bid for a specific contract or venture of limited duration which may not have implications of any further relationship between the companies involved. In the case of joint ventures, neither of these models is regarded as being a legal entity distinct from those companies participating in the venture. In other words, both or all companies presenting a bid will be treated as individually liable for any losses or responsibilities incurred during the planning and execution of the joint venture. Since these ventures do not exist as a separate legal entity, they are governed more by the agreements put in place between the participating companies than by outside government regulations. It is, therefore, absolutely essential to have good legal advice when establishing a joint venture in Argentina. Everything has to be agreed in fine detail before the bid is launched.

The procedure for establishing a joint venture between two or more companies is, from the regulatory point of view, simple - as follows:

● The companies must prepare and execute a private or public agreement between them governing all aspects of their rights and responsibilities for the execution of any joint commercial activities. It must be very specific with regard to the purpose of the venture, financing of the proposed activity (including details of where such financing is coming from), who will be legally responsible within the companies for the execution of any business and how long the Articles agreed between the companies will apply to their joint activities.

● The Agreement must be registered with the IGJ or appropriate Provincial authority. Franchises are protected under Argentine commercial laws. It is largely up to the franchiser to ensure that their rights are fully stated in the Franchise Agreement and that full advantage is taken of all legal protection on offer in the delicate matter of transfer of knowledge, know-how, intellectual property, copyright, trade marks, patented materials, etc.

Warning - It is essential that any franchising or licensing agreements are registered with any appropriate authorities for the industry if you wish to take advantage of any tax concessions available on royalties etc. Failure to do so may mean you or your franchise paying more tax than you need to! This is real 'legal eagle' country and you must take the advice of a recognised lawyer in this field, as recommended by your embassy or trade organisation.

Sole Proprietorship

This is known as an *empresa unipersonal*. The essential feature of this kind of business is that there are no partners involved. On the other hand, the sole proprietor must obey all the laws governing commerce which apply to any other kind of business and bears full and unlimited liability for the running of the company, the financial affairs of the company and the debts of the company. A foreign resident in Argentina is allowed to have this kind of company registered but if a foreigner is a non-resident in Argentina and wishes to establish this sort of company they must appoint an Argentine resident as their legal representative. This will require a legal contract between the two individuals being agreed.

Warning - this sort of company is highly dangerous. Though it gives you complete autonomy is also makes you liable, without limit, for any and all company debts and obligations. Your assets are 100 per cent at risk!

Partnerships

A partnership is called a *sociedad* and, apart from the standard SRL model (*see* above, Limited Liability Company) there are four other varieties of partnership which are recognised under the commercial and legal code.

7

Partnerships

These variations of partnership are not so commonly formed by or including foreign investors since they offer neither the protection or advantages afforded by the SA or SRL models. For instance, a general partnership agreement, or *Sociedad Colectiva* as it is known, makes all partners liable both jointly and severally for the company's liabilities. There are also some unattractive legislative requirements associated with this form of partnership, such as the need for a unanimous resolution requirement to change the original agreement. With the *Sociedad en Comandita* model of limited partnership the essential feature is that it allows for two kinds of partners being involved in the company. One variety invests in the form of a capital contribution but plays no active part in the running of the business – a silent partner. Their liability is limited to the amount of their investment only. The other variety of partner in this model is active in the running of the business but their liability is unlimited. The *Sociedad en Comandita* can take two distinct forms. The *Sociedad en Comandita por Acciones (SCA)* is similar to the SA model in that the partners hold shares in the company, all of which are of the same value. The second form, the *Sociedad en Comandita Simple* (SCS) is more similar to the SRL model in that the partner's capital is in equal amounts but is not held as shares. Setting up either of these models is similar in procedure to setting up an SA or SRL company and they are subject to similar regulatory regimes.

Useful addresses

Office of the Inspector General of Justice (IGJ)
Inspección General de Justicia (IGJ) San Martín 665
1004 Buenos Aires
❑ Tel: +54 1 312 2427; fax: +54 1 313 7609

National Security Commission (CNV)
Comisión Nacional de Valores (CNV)
Av. 25 de Mayo
175 1002 Buenos Aires

7

Buenos Aires

8

Buenos Aires

The nation's capital

Buenos Aires is one of the biggest and most fascinating cities in the Western Hemisphere. Built on the southern side of the great River Plate it stretches as far as the eye can see and covers a huge area. The land is a flat pancake with no natural boundaries apart from the river. The city has evolved over the centuries into an urban sprawl which now covers 123 sq. kms. for the Federal District alone. The Metropolitan Districts nucleus now rumbles over 1,800 sq. km. and contains over 12 million people. That is over one third of the entire Argentine population, which makes Buenos Aires by a long distance the most important city in the Republic and indeed anywhere south of Sao Paulo in Brazil and Lima in Peru. Many would argue, with some reason, that is the most important city in all South America. It is certainly the most cultured and European in outlook and appearance.

Over three million *Porteños* (People of the Port) as the citizens of Buenos Aires are known - and indeed call themselves with some pride - live crammed up mostly in small to medium sized apartments in the Federal District along the banks of the muddy-brown, slow-moving river. Those who live in the leafier suburbs usually work in the downtown centre, referred to as the *microcentro* and commute considerable distances using the excellent metro system and the frequent train and bus links. They all have in common one trait which becomes immediately obvious to the visitor – an immense pride in their beloved Buenos Aires.

Beginnings

Buenos Aires did not get off to a good start (*see* Chapter 1). It was not really until the nineteenth century that the city achieved dominance. When Charles Darwin passed through in 1883 he found the city "large, and I should think one of the most regular in the world. Every street is at the right angles to the one it crosses, and the parallel ones being equidistant, the houses are collected into solid squares of equal dimensions, which are called '*cuadras*'."

A modern day visitor to Buenos Aires will recognise instantly this grid layout, familiar in North American cities too (*cuadra* means block in Spanish). The 60,000 *Porteños* of Darwin's day of course lived in a much

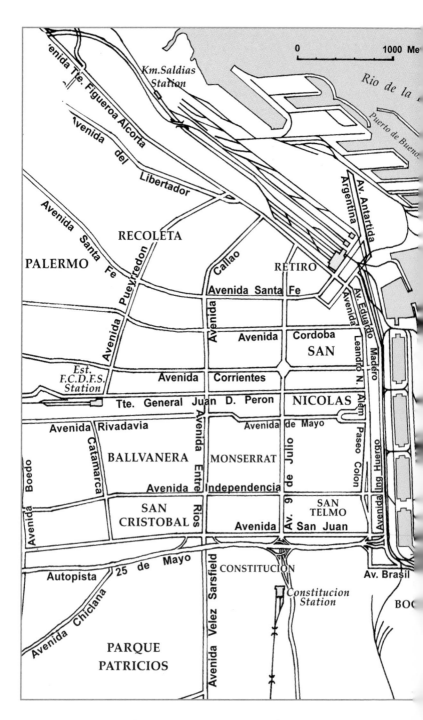

Buenos Aires City Centre

smaller city but today's citizens would still recognise this street pattern spreading out from the Plaza de Mayo on the banks of the river.

After independence from Spain the population grew steadily until by 1870 the city had tripled in size from Darwin's day. The next thirty years saw an explosive increase in immigration so that by the 1890s over half a million people, mostly recently arrived from Europe, inhabited the booming and increasingly sophisticated capital. By the beginning of the twentieth century Buenos Aires had over a million citizens and was the largest and most important city in South America.

In 1880 Buenos Aires changed from a city to a Federal District and was recognised as the undisputed centre of political, economic and social life in Argentina. Today little remains of the city before the nineteenth century. What we see now in the centre are *Porteño* versions of the ornate and beatiful boulevards which were so fashionable in the French capital at the time. The stone buildings with their shallow, exquisitely decorated balconies overlooking wide tree-lined streets are a monument to the taste of the city dwellers and architects who presided over the building boom in the *Belle Epoque*. Buenos Aires is still often referred to as 'the Paris of Latin America'. It is easy to see why.

8

During the 1930s much of the old colonial heart of the capital was ripped out and replaced with modern thoroughfares such as Corrientes, Santa Fé and Córdoba in order to ease access to the centre for the teeming populace occupying the ever-expanding suburbs. The housing built to accommodate these later waves of poor immigrants was less attractive than their predecessors and some areas have now degenerated into a featureless urban sprawl, sadly so typical of other great cities in South America.

To appreciate the development of Buenos Aires, it is best to put on some comfortable walking shoes and take a morning or afternoon off to walk around.Crossing the street is extremely dangerous and the traffic is unlikely to stop for you just because the lights happen to change. Be careful that traffic has stopped before stepping off the kerb.

Red de Metro

The Plaza de Mayo

Perhaps the best place to start in understanding the city is the Plaza de Mayo (May Square) outside the Casa Rosada (Pink House) where the president of the Republic has his office. The Plaza de Mayo has been at the heart of Buenos Aires and Argentine history since a small fortress was constructed there in 1580. Whenever *Porteños* in their long history have wanted to celebrate or to protest, they head straight for the great square. It is still the political and administrative centre of the Republic. On one side is the Presidential House, an imposing building built in 1894 but painted an interesting salmon pink. It is flanked by other key centres of power, the city Cathedral, the Town Council offices (*Cabildo*) and the National Bank of Argentina (equivalent to the Federal Reserve Bank or the Bank of England).

Today the Plaza de Mayo is a pleasant square where *Porteños* stroll or lounge on the benches under the tall palm trees and by the flower beds. It has, however, been far from a peaceful place over the centuries.

Where the Casa Rosada now stands was a wooden fortress to protect the first colonist from Indian attacks - a fairly frequent event in the sixteenth century. As the colony expanded, the space outside the fort became more a meeting place for the citizens to socialise and trade. Throughout the eighteenth century it became known as the Plaza del Mercado (Market Square). Briefly in 1807 the *Porteños* renamed it Plaza de la Victoria (Victory Square) in honour of their citizens' militia having foiled the British military invasion of their city. Finally, after independence from Spain, it became the Plaza de Mayo after the month in 1810 when independence was declared.

The Plaza de Mayo is where the dictator Rosas hung his victims to cow the populace into submission. It was here that Evita Perón marched with over 200,000 workers to protest at the imprisonment of her husband and force his early release. From the balcony of the Casa Rosada, Evita would sway masses thronging the Plaza below with her rousing speeches. In 1982, the populace spontaneously swarmed into the Plaza to celebrate the taking of the Malvinas (Falklands) by the Galtieri government. Less than three months later, when the

8

Plaza de Mayo

truth about the war was out in the open, they were back again wanting to drag him out of the Casa Rosada by force if necessary

Argentina's two World Cup football triumphs have seen the square packed with proud ecstatic *Porteños*. Nearly a million of them headed for the Plaza de Mayo in 1987 to show the military that they would not put up with their supporting a right-wing attempted coup by some extremists in their ranks (*see* the *Carapintada* episode in Chapter 1).

The most famous visitors to the Plaza are the Mothers of the Plaza de Mayo who still protest every Thursday in front of the Casa Rosada at the loss of their relatives in *Mothers of the Plaza* the Dirty War in the 1970s. Many are pensioners now *de Mayo* but rain or shine they still don't their famous white headscarves and walk through the Plaza to remind everyone who cares to listen that their disappeared loved ones are not forgotten.

Buenos Aires is a beautiful city and worth getting to know. More details and the sights of the capital can be found in Chapter 10.

Eating and Drinking

Up-Market

General notes on food and Argentine eating habits are covered in Chapter 3. Here, however, are listed a few specific restaurants worthy of recommendation.

Clarks
Sarmiento 645
❏ Tel: (11) 4325 3624.
English-style restaurant fittings and feel. The place to be seen, especially lunchtime, as well as to eat well. Drinks are rather expensive. Standard Argentine and international style menu.

Au Bec Fin
Vicente López 1825
❏ Tel: (11) 4801 6894.
Long established, very formal. International and French cuisine a speciality.

Munich Recoleta
RM Ortiz 1871
❏ Tel: (11) 4804 4469.
International menu, German specialities.

Cabana Las Lilas
Alicia Moreau de Justo 516
❏ Tel: (11) 4313-1336.
In the renovated, chic Puerto Madero development of dockside wharves and warehouses, this one is for devout carnivores and red wine lovers. Very stylish and surprisingly intimate atmosphere.

Puerto Cristal
Alicia Moreau de Justo 1082
❏ Tel: (11) 4331 3309.
In the Puerto Madero development. International cuisine with home-made pastas. Excellent fish and seafood.

Midori
Posadas 1232
❏ Tel: (11) 4814 5151
Inside the five star Caesar Park Hotel, this is the finest Japanese restaurant in town and the best in South America outside the Japanese Quarter in Sao Paulo Brazil. Distinctly expensive!

Morena
Rafael Obligado y Pampa - Costanera Norte
❏ Tel: (11) 4786 0204
One of several fine international cuisine restaurants near the Aeroparque with open vistas over the river.

Charlies Fondue
Av. Libertador 15.900 San Isidro
❏ Tel: (11) 4747 4709
Situated in the elegant northern suburb of San Isidro about 30 to 40 minutes from the centre. Intimate atmosphere, Swiss cuisine.

Middle Range
La Etancia
Lavalle 941
❏ Tel: (11) 4326 0330
Don't be put off by the touristy display of an open fire with goat or kid roasting on upright spits around an open fire in the front window and waiters dressed like overweight *gauchos* milling around inside. This is one of the best *parrilla* restaurants in town.

8

El Palacio De La Papa Frita
Lavalle 737 and 954
❑ Tel: (11) 4393 5849
There are four of these restaurants in Buenos Aires, two
in Lavalle. Absolutely typical *Porteños* restaurants, long
and narrow from the street. Very professional waiters in
black tie and white jackets. Pages and pages of Argentine
menu specialising in beef (what else!) but accompanied by
the finest soufflé potatoes you are likely to find
anywhere. For potato fans, it is a must!

Los Immortales
Lavalle 748
❑ Tel: (11) 4322 5493
Also another restaurant on Av.Corrientes 1369. Strong
atmosphere of Argentina in the classic age of the Tango.
Extensive menu, Argentine and Italo-Argentine dishes.
Excellent pizzas and cannelloni. Highly professional service.

La Mosca Blanca
Av. Ramos Mejía 1430
❑ Tel: 4313 4890
Tucked away to the side of the Retiro railway station,
this restaurant has a wide variety of superb Argentine
meat and fish dishes served in very generous portions.
This author recalls a particularly fine fillet of sole in blue
Roquefort cheese sauce! Dont' be put off by the name
(the White Fly) – the food is delicious!

Los Tronquitos
Av.51 Esquina 122
❑ Tel: (11) 4212 187
Typical Argentine *Parrilla* meat restaurant. Simple food
but excellent prime material, well prepared.

Rincon Hispano
Av. Alvarez Jonte 2599 esq. Bolivia.
❑ Tel: (11) 4582 0593
About 15 minutes from the centre, specialises in Spanish
food, particularly Mediterranean style, fish and seafood.
Flamenco show on Mondays.

Economic end
Sandwiches, *empanadas* and other snacks are widely
available in *Confiterias* which serve light food and drinks
Confiterias are also the place to go to enjoy cakes of all
varieties. *Porteños* have a notoriously sweet tooth and a

8

fine tradition in pastries, cakes and icecreams. Freddos, a chain of outlets, offers a magnificent variety of ice creams if you fancy cooling down on a hot summers day.

Between Viamonte and Av. Córdoba on the pedestrian-only stretch of Florida is a shopping mall called *Galerías Pacifico*. On the lower level there is a variety of good fast food outlets which provide simple, fast meals for under US$10 including a drink.

La Casa China
Viamonte 1476
❏ Tel: (11) 4371 1352
Good fixed price lunch menu at under US$10.

Pizzeria Serafin
Av. Corrientes 1328
❏ Tel: (11) 4371 2666.
Typical Buenos Aires style Italian restaurant.

Big Mamma
Cabello 3760
❏ Tel: (11) 4806 6822
Also at Matienzo 1599 Tel:4772 0926. Exotic hot and cold sandwiches, bagels etc. Upmarket fast-food not unlike a New York delicatessen.

8

Many downtown pubs offer an Executive Menu at lunchtime for around US$10-15. Among the best for a bite and a drink are:

Downtown Matias
San Martín 979
❏ Tel: (11) 4312 9844
Also at Reconquista 704. Irish pub and restaurant, informal atmosphere open for lunch only during working week, open all evenings including weekends.

The Temple Bar
Marcelo T. Alvear 495
❏ Tel: (11) 4322 0474
Irish Pub. Executive menu, Happy Hours, occasional live music.

Druid Inn
Reconquista 1040
❏ Tel: (11) 4312 3688
Traditional Irish dishes and snacks. A superb selection of whiskies and beers.

Hotels

Luxury Hotels: US$ 250+

Alvear Palace Hotel ★★★★★
Av. Alvear 1891
❑ Tel: (11) 808 2100; fax: (11) 804 9246
Older hotel in the Paris Ritz mode built in 1920s. Handy for embassies and chic shopping but 15 minutes from downtown by cab in fashionable Barrio Norte.

Cesar Park Buenos Aires ★★★★★
Posadas 1232, Recoleta
❑ Tel: (11) 814 5150; fax: (11) 814 5148
Located in one of the best dining out areas of the capital. All the usual trimmings and swimming pool.

Crowne Plaza Panamericano ★★★★★
Carlos Pellegrini 525
❑ Tel: (11) 4348 5000; fax: (11) 4348 5251
Conveniently located for business and leisure activities.

Hotel Libertador Kempinski Buenos Aires ★★★★★
Av. Córdoba 680
❑ Tel: (11) 4322 2095
Modern and bright, near downtown business and shopping.

Hotel Plaza Francia ★★★★
Eduardo Schiaffino 2189
❑ Tel: (11) 4804 9631; fax: (11) 4804 9631
Near Recoleta for wining and dining. Good access to downtown or Barrio Norte.

Inter-Continental Hotel ★★★★★
Moreno 809
❑ Tel: (11) 340 7100; fax: (11) 340 7199
Five years old. Usual Intercontinental chain facilitiies. Swimming Pool.

Marriott Plaza Hotel ★★★★★
Florida 1005
❑ Tel: (11) 318 3000; fax: (11) 313 2912
Right on the pedestrian section of Florida Street, the heartland of downtown shopping. Handy for cinemas, theatre and nightlife.

Sheraton Hotel Buenos Aires ★★★★★
San Martín
Retiro
❑ Tel: (11) 318 9000; fax: (11) 318 9353

8

Located near the riverside, across the park from the Retiro railway and bus centre. Beautiful night-time views from penthouse bar. Large modern tower. Usual Sheraton facilities. A bit isolated at night but easy to get to by cab. Convenient for embassies and Florida Street shopping area.

Claridge Hotel ★★★★★
Tucumán 535
❏ Tel: (11) 314 2020; fax: (11) 322 8022
As the name implies, older English style hotel. Well located in downtown on noisy but central street in San Nicolás near Florida shopping street. Excellent bar and restaurant.

Middle Range: $100 -150+
Continental Hotel ★★★★
Av. Roque Saenz Peña 725
❏ Tel: (11) 326 1700; fax: (11) 322 1421
Off Florida Street. Quiet, older style hotel but tastefully modernised.

Conquistador Hotel ★★★★
Suipacha 948
❏ Tel: (11) 4328 3012; fax: (11) 4328 3252
Centrally located for business and shopping, features rooftop restaurant

8

Gran Hotel Colón ★★★★
Carlos Pellegrini 507
❏ Tel: (11) 4320 3500; fax: (11) 4320 3507
In the heart of the city near the obelisk – so you can find your way easily enough! Well appointed rooms but some traffic noise.

Hotel Lafayette ★★★★
Reconquista 546
❏ Tel: (11) 4393 9081; fax: (11) 4393 9081
Centrally located downtown near shopping streets.

Under US$100
Esmeralda Palace Hotel ★★★★
Esmeralda 527
❏ Tel: (11) 4393 1085; fax: (11) 4393 1185
Just off corner of Lavalle, near Florida. Handy for cinemas, dining and shopping. Air-conditioned, but the internal rooms can be small and rather dark. Rooms $75+.

Gran Hotel Argentino ★★★
Carlos Pellegrini 37
❏ Tel: (11) 4334 4001; fax: (11) 4334 4001
Handy for Microcentre. Rooms vary from around $60+.

Hotel Lyon
Riobamba 251
❏ Tel: (11) 4372 0100; fax: (11) 4814 4252
Spacious rooms. Friendly staff. Rooms from $70+.

Hotel Plaza Roma
Lavalle 110
❏ Tel: (11) 4314 0666; fax: (11) 4312 0839
Near Puerta Madero development of modern restaurants on dockside. Rooms from $60+.

Hotel Phoenix
San Martín 780
❏ Tel: (11) 4312 4845; fax: (11) 4311 2846
What was once a beautiful but fading hotel has risen once more, like its name, to something like its former glories. An interesting and tasteful blend of old and new. Rooms from $75+.

Economic hotels:
Hotel Americano
Rodriguez Peña 265
❏ Tel: (11) 4382 4229; fax: (11) 4382 4229
In Congreso. Older style but remodelled. Rooms $45.

Hotel El Cabildo
Lavalle 748
❏ Tel: (11) 4322 6695; fax: (11) 43226695
In Microcentro. Handy for business and shopping. A bit basic. Rooms $40+.

Hotel Orense
Bartolomé Mitre 1359
Air conditioned. Near Congress building. Rooms $30+.

Tucumán Palace Hotel
Tucumán 384
❏ Tel: (11) 4311 2298; fax: (11) 4311 2296
Central location but noisy street. Rooms $45+.

8

9

other Cities

other cities

Although Buenos Aires dominates Argentina in terms of population, wealth and political power there are several other cities which play a major role in the Argentine economy.

Rosario

Traditionally the second city of Argentina -a title hotly disputed with Córdoba - Rosario lies in Santa Fé Province on the River Paraná, 300 kms. north of Buenos Aires (just under an hour's flying time). The city has around one million inhabitants and was originally a port for the collection and shipping of grain and the reception of agricultural workers into the country. Despite its distance well up the Paraná River it is quite capable of taking ocean-going vessels. It has become a very important industrial centre at the heart of major road and rail networks. Oddly, it is not the administrative capital of the province, a status still residing in the much smaller city of Santa Fé further upstream.

Rosario is laid out on the traditional grid pattern with the Plaza 25 de Mayo as its heart. The city was established c.1720 and grew up towards the end of the last century as agricultural activity expanded. Commercial activity is centred on the pedestrian-only streets of San Martín and Córdoba.

9

Apart from some French architecture similar to that found in Buenos Aires there is little of architectural note. The most famous landmark is the *Monumento Nacional de la Bandera* (National Monument of the Flag) at the end of Calle Córdoba. The huge mausoleum is shaped like a boat and covers 10,000 sq.m. It contains the tomb of General Belgrano (the designer of the flag of the Republic), and the original flag itself. Since it is topped by a tower almost 80 metres high, it is hard to miss and serves as an excellent point to get your bearings. It is open daily from 7 a.m. to 7 p.m. except on Mondays when it is closed in the mornings.

The city boasts some fine views of the river and south-west of the downtown areas lies the extensive Parque Independencia (Independent Park) which is where the Rosarinos go to relax and enjoy the open air.

Eating and Drinking

La Rural
A. Pellegrini 1077
❏ Tel: (341) 4812 159
Argentine menu.

Il Piccolo Navio
San Luis 709
❏ Tel: (341) 4488 557
Italian and international food

La Estancia
Wheelwright 1781
❏ Tel: (341) 4499 562

Hemingway Restaurante
Av. Belgrano y Rioja
❏ Tel: (341) 4492 626
International cuisine. Fronts onto the river.

Hotels

Ariston ★★★★
Córdoba 2554
❏ Tel: (341)425 8666; fax: 425 9142
Good location for business. Rooms $80+

Hotel Libertador ★★★★
Córdoba and Corrientes
❏ Tel: (341) 24 1005
100 rooms. One of the best hotels in town. Rooms $80+.

Hotel Republica ★★★
San Lorenzo 955
❏ Tel: (341) 424 8351; fax: 424 8760
Near business area and parks. Rooms $60+.

Hotel Rosario ★★★★
Cortada Ricardone 1365
❏ Tel: (341) 424 2170; fax: 424 6677
74 Rooms. Rooms $80+.

Córdoba

The province of Córdoba and the city lie in the centre of
the most populated provinces of the Republic. Long
before Buenos Aires attained political and economic
supremacy, Córdoba was an important political,
administrative and educational centre. Located in the

foothills of the Andes, at a point where the peaks are less formidable, it sits on the south bank of the Rio Primero and was founded by de Cabrera in 1573.

From its very beginning it was also an important base for the missionary activities of the Church and still boasts many fine religious buildings from colonial times. It is now home to around 1.25 million inhabitants and has become an important industrial centre, especially in the making of automobiles, though that is now on decline.

The focal point of the city is the Plaza San Martín. The *Cabildo* (Town Council Offices) on the Plaza is a noble example of colonial architecture as is the cathedral, begun in the second half of the sixteenth century, on the Southwest corner of the Plaza. Two blocks from the cathedral on Calle Caseros is the Jesuit Complex, housing a fine collection of religious buildings from the seventeenth and eighteenth centuries.

The colonial heart of the city is all around the Plaza and a walk down Calle Obispo Trejo south of the Plaza contains some of the finest architectural examples of those days. The University of Córdoba at number 242 is a must. Built between 1613 and 1621, it is the oldest building in Argentina. The Calle leads to the Parque Sarmiento which provides a welcome relief from the tightly packed urban centre.

The business area of Córdoba is north-west of the Plaza San Martín at the intersection of Indarte and 25 de Mayo. The city's largest park, the Parque General San Martín, is also located on the banks of the river in this area. Most of the industrial belt is south of the central area.

Eating and Drinking

La Alameda
Obispo Trejo 170
Traditional local dishes

Emir
Boulevard Illia 71
International and Arab cuisine

Hamster
P.Lugones
International and German food

9

Hotels

César C. Carman ★★★★
Av. Sabattini 439
❑ Tel: (51) 34516
Next to Sarmiento Park. Rooms $80+.

Gran Savoy Hotel ★★★
Jerónimo de Cabrera 201
❑ Tel: (51) 471 8050; fax: (51) 471 6707
60 rooms. Rooms $60+.

Hotel Panorama
Marcelo T. Alvear 251
❑ Tel: (51) 4420 4000; fax: (51) 420 3900
146 Rooms. Swimming Pool. Rooms $120+.

Sheraton Córdoba Hotel ★★★★★
Av. Duarte Quiróz 1300
❑ Tel: (51)488 9000; fax: (51)488 9150
Only Five Star in town. Typical Sheraton. Rooms $150+.

Sussex Hotel
San Jerónimo 125
❑ Tel: (51) 229071; fax: (51) 229070
Classic hotel with 110 rooms. Rooms $80+.

Windsor Hotel ★★★★
Buenos Aires 214 corner with Entre Rios
❑ Tel: (51) 422 4012; fax: (51) 422 4015
Smaller hotel. Rooms $80+.

Mendoza

This provincial capital is high in the Andes, over 750 metres above sea level, and was founded in 1561. It is named after a Spanish governor of what is now Chile and for the first two centuries of its existence had stronger ties with Chile than with Argentina. The city stands near a pass through the Andes to Santiago de Chile. Mendoza is now home to over 700,000 Argentines and has not only a rich cultural past and a fine university, but is also an important administrative and industrial centre.

If you are lucky enough to be visiting in March you can visit the Wine Vintage Festival, although the city is full of bodegas (wine cellars) where you can sample the excellent wines of the Cuyo region (the provinces of Mendoza, San Luis and San Juan) all year round. Argentina is the fifth largest wine producing country in the world and

Mendoza has well over a thousand wineries. Only in the last few decades has their excellent wine been exported on a large scale outside South America.

The Plaza Independencia is the focal point of the city. Smaller plazas surround the main plaza and one of them, the Plaza España, has an interesting handicraft market on Saturday mornings. The main thoroughfare running north-south is the Avenida San Martín, and is a useful reference point for strolling through the centre and also contains many banks and money exchanges.

Eating and Drinking

Pizzas y Pastas
Arístides Villanueva 451
❑ Tel: (61) 4220 586
Italian food of course !

Charles Dickens Pub
Arístides Villanueva 290
❑ Tel: (61) 4240 847
Confitería. Sandwiches, snacks and drinks in English pub atmosphere.

Hotels

Crillon Hotel ★★★
Per 1065
❑ Tel: (61) 423 8963; fax: (61) 423 9658
Rooms $50+.

Gran Hotel ★★★★
Huentala Primitivo de la Reta 1007
❑ Tel: (61) 4200 802/941; fax: (61) 4200 604
Rooms $60+.

Gran Hotel Mendoza ★★★
Av. España 1210
❑ Tel: (61) 425 2000; fax: (61) 425 2523
80 rooms. Rooms $50+.

Hotel Aconcagua ★★★★
San Lorenzo 545
❑ Tel: (61) 24 2321; fax: (61) 31 1085
Well located for business purposes. Rooms $70+.

Plaza Hotel ★★★★
Chile 1124
❑ Tel: (61) 4233 000; fax: (61) 4233 000
80 Rooms. Rooms $60+.

9

La Plata

This is the Provincial Capital of Buenos Aires Province and was built in the 1880s to house the Provincial legislature when Buenos Aires City became the Federal capital of the whole Republic. It now has some 600,000 inhabitants and though only 56 km. south-east of the capital, it has its own distinct life played out on the grid pattern of civic construction beloved of the 1880s. Built in the grandiose style of the period the public buildings are clustered around the Plaza Moreno whereas the business centre is based around the nearby Plaza San Martín. The city also houses a large and prestigious university, a zoo bigger than that of Buenos Aires and an important Natural History Museum.

Eating and Drinking

A Tavola
Calle 11 857
❏ Tel: (221) 4230 692
Italian and Italo-Argentine dishes.

El Colonial
Calle 10 Esquina 40
❏ Tel: (221) 4210 223
Argentine Menu.

Comidas Arabes
Calle 57 y Diagonal 73
❏ Tel: (221) 4227 593
Arabic Specialities.

Los Hermanos
Camino Centenario y 11
❏ Tel: (221) 4802 539
Parrilla Restaurant

Los Tronquitos
Av 51 Esquina 122
❏ Tel: (221) 4212 187
Parrilla Restaurant.

Hotels

Note: Since La Plata is only 64 kilometers from Buenos Aires and has regular trains every half hour it is perfectly feasible to visit La Plata on a daily basis from your hotel base in Buenos Aires.

9

Hotel Corregidor ★★★★
Calle 6 Number 1026
☐ Tel: (221) 425 6800; fax: 425 6805
The only four star hotel. Rooms $100+.

Hotel Catedral ★★★
Calle 49 Number 965
☐ Tel: (221) 423 2010; fax 483 0091
27 Rooms. Rooms $50+.

Hotel San Marco ★★★
Calle 54 Number 523
☐ Tel: (221) 422 9322; fax: 422 9322
60 Rooms. Rooms $50+.

Mar del Plata

The seaside playground for the millions from Buenos Aires and surrounding provinces who flock there every year for their long summer holidays, this town sprang up when it was bought from its Portuguese owners in 1874 by an Argentine speculator called Patricio Peralta Ramos. He was successful in persuading wealthy *Porteños* to construct summer houses along the eight kilometres of sandy beachfront some 400 kms. south of the capital. There, the cooler Atlantic breezes meant they could escape the stifling humidity of the Buenos Aires summer months. The town grew considerably in the 1930s when a major casino is was built for the rich holidaymakers to enjoy. The casino is still a major attraction. Mar del Plata now has half a million permanent residents but the number quadruples during the hectic holiday season from October to May.

Some elegant summer houses remain in the Barrio Los Troncos but the rest of the city is a tightly packed collection of functional but architecturally unattractive highrise apartment blocks built in 1960s and 1970s with scant regard for aesthetic considerations. They were lapped up in a speculative frenzy to house the flood of middle-class holidaymakers who followed where their richer predecessors had led. These days the rich have moved on to quieter and more exclusive holiday resorts such as Punta del Este in Uruguay. The main beach is the Playa Grande and there is a variety of accommodation and restaurants throughout the city. Unless you are really into crowds and noise it is best avoided in the high season!

9

Eating and Drinking

As befits a seaside resort catering for an influx of nearly two million people a year there is no shortage of restaurants and pubs to suit all tastes and pockets.However, if you like seafood try:

La Forcheta
Almafuerte 247
Fresh and varied fish and seafood dishes, elegantly presented. Reasonably priced, pleasant atmosphere.

Hotels

As this is a holiday resort there is no shortage of hotels, Although many close out of season. There is a particular abundance of inexpensive three- and two Star hotels ranging in price from $30 - $60 a room depending on the season, but it is usually possible even in high season to find somewhere for a night or two

Costa Galana Hotel ★★★★★
Peralta Ramos 5725
❏ Tel: (223) 486 0000; fax: (223) 486 2020
Pure holiday luxury. Rooms $200+.

Sheraton Mar del Plata Hotel ★★★★★
Av. Alem 4221
❏ Tel: (223) 4999 000; fax: (223) 4999 009
Modern. All usual Sheraton chain facilities. Rooms $200+

Primacy ★★★★★
Santa Fe 2464
❏ Tel: (223) 491 3600/9; fax: (223) 491 3205
Intimate service, only 63 rooms. Rooms $200+.

Bisonte Hotel ★★★★
Belgrano 2601
❏ Tel: (223) 495 6028; fax: (223) 495 6060
80 Rooms. Rooms $120+.

Gran Hotel Iruña ★★★★
Av. Juan. B. Alberdi 2270
❏ Tel: (223) 4954 037/38; fax: (223) 491 2072
Larger style. 145 Rooms. Rooms $120+.

Provincial ★★★★
Boulevard Marítimo 2502
❏ Tel: (223) 495 24081
Near world-famous casino. Rooms $150+.

9

Gran Hotel Casino ★★★
Boulevard Marítimo 2300
❏ Tel: (223) 495 4011
Also near the casino. Rooms $70+.

Tucumán

Properly called San Miguel de Tucumán, this is the capital of the smallest province of Argentina but it has a historical and economic importance beyond its size. It was founded in 1565 by Spaniards who arrived from the other side of the Andes and is now home to over half a million inhabitants. The wealth of the area is founded in its well-watered and temperate climate where crops such as sugar are easily cultivated but it began life as a crossroads for the routes leading from Rosario, Córdoba and the agricultural producers of the east on the way north to Bolivia and beyond to Lima and, eventually, Spain.

Much of the old colonial city has been lost but it boasts an excellent Folklore Museum and the Casa Histórica (Historic House) on Calle Congreso 151. The original room in which the Declaration of Independence was signed in 1816 still stands, although the rest of the building has been largely rebuilt.

9

Eating and Drinking
La Nita
25 de Mayo 377
❏ Tel: 4229 196
Reasonably priced typical *parrilla* meat restaurant.

Jockey Club
San Martín 451
❏ Tel: 4213 946
International and Argentine dishes

Pekin
25 de Mayo 135
❏ Tel: 4215 598
Chinese menu.

Dulce Vita Tratoria
Maipú 790
❏ Tel: 4306 125
Italian, Italo-Argentine International cuisine

El Fogon
Marcos Paz 630
❏ Tel: 4217 535
Argentine and regional dishes

Hotels

Gran Hotel ★★★★★
Av. De los Próceres 380
❏ Tel: 424 5000; fax: 431 0324
Excellent Service. 143 rooms. Near 9 July Park. Rooms $120+.

Del Sol ★★★★
Laprida 35
❏ Tel: 431 1755; fax: 431 2010
100 rooms. Good location. Rooms $80+.

Metropol Swiss Hotel ★★★★
24 de Septiembre 524
❏ Tel: 431 1180; fax: 431 0379
Central location. 100 Rooms. Rooms $80+.

Presidente ★★★
Monteagudo 249
❏ Tel: 431 1414; fax: 431 1474
Friendly service. 50 rooms. Swimming pool. Rooms $60+.

Carlos V ★★★
25 de Mayo 330
❏ Tel: 431 1566; fax: 431 1666
70 Rooms. Rooms $60+.

9

a break from business

a break from business

Exploring Buenos Aires

A walking tour of Buenos Aires is probably the best way to get an insight into the city, its people and its history.

What follows is an appreciation of the city's main landmarks.

The Casa Rosada

Quite why this building is such a strange pink colour is a matter of some dispute. The colour was chosen by President Sarmiento and some *Porteños* say it was the only colour other than white available at the time and he did not want the building to be the same colour as its more famous counterpart in Washington. Others think he simply wanted a neutral colour which would not offend the two leading political parties of the day who had chosen red and white respectively as their emblems. Either way, the result is a very dull pink which is at odds with the rest of the buildings in the Plaza.

Inside the Casa Rosada is a small museum which contains mementos of some of the Argentine presidents and heroes who have occupied or visited the building since it was built in 1894. It is open every day except Wednesdays and Saturdays from 1100 to 1800.

The Casa Rosada is guarded by the Grenadier Regiment whose job it is also to guard the President and escort him on State duties. Originally a regiment in the armies of San Martín they still wear the magnificent uniforms of the cavalrymen of this day. They provide a mounted escort for the President and any visiting Head of State.

The Metropolitan Cathedral

The north-west corner of the Plaza is dominated by the city's cathedral. It is no surprise to find it side-by-side with the seat of political power influence on Argentine affairs. Even today some 90 per cent of Argentines profess to the Catholic faith although the political influence of the Church was waned considerably in the last two decades.

The building was completed only in 1827, it is not a particulary interesting church in terms of architecture but it does have some fine wood carvings and a few oil paintings possibly attributable to Rubens. It does, however, contain one very important tomb. The body of General San Martín was repatriated from England and now lies in a magnificent sarcophagus in a place of honour revered by all Argentines.

10

The Cabildo (Town Council Building)

This building occupies a special place in Argentine history. On this site the Town Councils of Buenos Aires have been meeting since the late sixteenth century and it was here that many of the meetings and decisions took place which led to eventual independence from Spain. The elegant building now occupying the site dates only from 1751 and originally occupied the entire western side of the Plaza. It contains a museum of the colonial period of Buenos Aires history which is open in the afternoons except on Saturdays and Mondays and on Sunday from 1500 to 1900.

The Banco de la Nación

This was built in 1888 and is an impressive example of the ornate and imposing architecture favoured by architects and politicians of the day. It is still the symbolic centre of the nation's wealth but in fact the day-to-day business of running the finances of the state are now conducted largely elsewhere in more modern offices throughout the city.

The Avenida de Mayo

At the Plaza de Mayo stop and admire the view down the Avenida de Mayo, an imposing boulevard built in 1894 linking the Presidential House in the Plaza and the Congress of the Deputies at its other extreme. It is a long walk, fifteen blocks, but worth it to get a feel for the heart of the city. After ten blocks you reach the Avenida 9 de Julio which may be the widest street in the world, almost 150m. from sidewalk to sidewalk. To cross it other than at the designated places would be suicidal.

The most striking feature and an unmissable city landmark is the obelisk (*el obelisco*) marking the intersection of the Avenida 9 de Julio and the Diagonal Norte. This was constructed in 1936 to commemorate the city's 400th anniversary. At 70 metres high, it is an excellent landmark if you lose your sense of direction.

The Plaza de los Dos Congresos (Square of the Two Congresses)

The monumental Victorian edifice housing the elected representatives of the people is at the end of your journey down the Avenida. Behind a pleasant municipal square you will find the imposing building which houses both

10

the Argentine Congress and Senate. It is still used as a debating chamber though much of the day-to-day work of the political leaders is done in modern buildings nearby.

The Plaza is not named after the two legislatures, but after two famous Congresses of the nineteenth century. It is also the zero kilometre mark for all maps in Argentina.

The Teatro Colón (Colón Opera House)

Undoubtedly the jewel in the crown of Argentine culture and one of the world's truly great opera houses and theatres is the Teatro Colón. It is an immense building occupying an entire block on Cerrito (part of Avenida 9 de Julio, which changes its name along its length)

Built in the grand style of late nineteenth century European opera houses, it was completed in 1907. It is a grandiose statement of how the *Porteños* of the day saw themselves, equal in wealth, culture and sophistication to their contemporaries in Paris, London and New York. It employs over 1,000 people and can entertain an audience of 3,500. The theatre is the centre of Argentine cultural life for opera, ballet and classical music.

Throughout the season (April-November) it hosts the very best of European and American performers as well as mounting splendid works and concerts by Argentina's own National Symphony Orchestra and National Ballet. To sit in the plush velvet seating or look up and admire the ornate chandeliers while being entertained by some of the world's greatest music played by the world's finest artists is truly an unforgettable experience. Get tickets if you can!

If you cannot get to a performance then a tour of the building is also worthwhile. Apart from Sundays there are hourly guided tours between 9 a.m. and 4 p.m., except on Saturday when tours ends at midday.

Lavalle and Florida

The best way to savour the atmosphere and variety of Buenos Aires is to walk down the two main pedestrianised streets in the heart of downtown. It is a long walk but well worth it! Beginning where Lavalle meets 9 de Julio (opposite the Teatro Colón) you will eventually come to the intersection with Florida. At this

10

Lavalle

point Lavalle ceases to be pedestrian only. This first section of Lavalle is filled with cinemas and restaurants and is often teeming with *Porteños* until the early hours of the morning. At times it is difficult to work your way through the queues for the cinemas and the crush of people out for a meal or simply an evening stroll. Together with Avenida Corrientes, it is the heart of the entertainment district of the city and off the sidestreets are many more theatres, nightclubs, cinemas and cafés. Lavalle is rather brash and garish but contains some good places to browse for souvenirs or cheap music CDs.

Florida

Lavalle is outdone in stylishness by Florida. The Florida shops are more sophisticated and, of course, more expensive. Dotted down the length of the street are small kiosks which sell a wide variety of national and international newspapers and magazines as well as paperbacks, maps and tourist guides to the city. Others offer flowers, candies, tobacco and souvenirs. By the time you stroll down to the end of Avenida Florida and encounter the elegant San Martín Square in front of the sumptious Foreign Office building you are in serious designer goods territory. The crowd will have thinned and the chic ladies and gentlemen of Buenos Aires can be seen meandering unhurriedly in and out of the boutiques and specialists shops on either side of the street. It is easy to imagine you are in Paris or Milan.

Plaza San Martín

When you reach the Plaza San Martín, which is on a small hill, take a few moments to rest under the jacarandas and palm trees and admire the view over the Retiro area with the river beyond. Below you to the left is the Retiro railway station where key suburban trainlines stretch out into the wealthy northern suburbs. Between the station and the Sheraton hotel stands a clocktower with a clockface similar to that of Big Ben in London. This was built as part of the municipal park by the British residents of Buenos Aires but the park has been renamed the Air Force Plaza since the Malvinas conflict.

Recoleta

If you still have the energy, a gentle stroll of some twenty-five minutes or so through some of the most elegant streets of the capital brings you the Recoleta area with its famous cemetery. If you are there on a Sunday head for the biggest crafts fair in Buenos Aires held in the nearby

10

Plaza Francia, if not go straight to the area bordering the cemetery where you will find some of the most elegant citizens sipping aperitif or coffee in the numerous chic cafés and restaurants facing the cemetery walks.

The Grave of Eva Perón

There is one body considered by some a cuckoo in the nest amongst the aristocratic families at rest in the cemetary of Recoleta – that of Eva Duarte Perón. Evita's odyssey leading to her final resting place was one of the most bizarre stories of modern political times. On her death, her husband took the highly unusual step of having her body embalmed. Preserved in this way, Evita became almost a Lenin-like icon for the poor of the nation, so much so that when her husband fell from power in 1955 General Aramburu had her body snatched and smuggled out of the country to an obscure grave in a Milan cemetery. From there, Evita was removed to a chapel in the house in Madrid where her husband spent his exile. So potent was the myth and legend surrounding Evita that it was not until the 1970s that General Lanusse allowed the return of the body to its native soil. Aramburu was not forgiven by the radical Peronists. He was kidnapped and murdered by the *Montoneros* in 1970. They refused to hand over his body for burial until Evita's was back in Buenos Aires. Ironically, the right-wing General and the left-wing heroine now lie only a few yards from each other. It is easy to find Evita's tomb – fresh flowers are placed there every day by her admirers.

10

This astonishing cemetery is the necropolis for the great and the good, and not a few who were far from either, of the Republic. There are guided tours available from early morning until six at night but you are allowed to enter on your own if you prefer. To wander through the lanes between the mausoleums is to understand the wealth and exclusiveness of the Argentine society which governed the city and the nation during its heyday. Most of the great Argentine families, many who have assumed the Presidency at one time or another are buried here. The Sarmientos, Mitres and Avellanedas all have their vaults in this elegant testament to Argentine wealth and power.

Museo Nacional de Bellas Artes (National Fine Arts Museum)

Just north of the Recoletas cemetery at Avenida del Libertador 1473 is Argentina's most important collection of paintings and sculptures. Apart from Mondays, it opens every afternoon until 7.30 p.m. and all day on Saturday. It houses not only the best of Argentine art from the last two centuries but also some fine works by Renoir, Picasso, Rodin and Monet.

Palermo and Palermo Chico

Beyond Recoletas on either side of the great Avenida Libertador lies what has always been one of the most pleasant and exclusive areas of the city. One visitor to the area a hundred years ago wrote: "Nowhere in the world does one get a stronger impression of exuberant wealth and extravagance". The park itself, called Palermo, lies on the edge of the city towards the river. It provides a breathing space for the citizens of today as much as it did for their predecessors. It is now somewhat less exclusive and elegant than in its prime but still encompasses the city's zoo, botanical gardens, polo ground, race track and a planetarium.

10

Nestling in this privileged area, the winding streets of Palermo Chico are still a district inhabited by the rich and famous. Many of the elegant mansions built during the *Belle Epoque* are no longer owned by the aristocratic families who built them but have become embassies or official offices. The area retains a lived-in air and is still regarded as a highly desirable address.

Barrio San Telmo

Take a taxi for the Plaza de Mayo southwards along Calle Defensa to San Telmo. Ask for Dorrego where the Bolivar and Humberto streets meet. This *barrio* (municipal district or neighbourhood) has a long and chequered history. It started life in the eighteenth century as a trading post and resting place for merchants on their way to the Plaza del Mercado, as the Plaza de Mayo then was, from the ships offloading at Riochuelo south of the city. A community of innkeepers, restaurateurs and small shopkeepers grew up to attend to the needs of these merchants. It was by all accounts a lawless community where drink and other pleasures were easily obtained. By the next century, however, it improved as wealthier families moved into the area to do business and bring order. They built many of the narrow-fronted town houses still to be seen in San Telmo today.

A terrible epidemic of yellow fever swept the area in the 1870s and convinced all who could afford it to leave unhealthy riverside air for the new northern and western suburbs. They were replaced over the next two decades by the great influx of European immigrants, mainly from Italy and Spain, which turned the town houses into overcrowded and insanitary tenements. It remained a poor and unfashionable area of the city until the 1960s when artists, intellectuals and hippies began to move into the crumbling but historic buildings to enjoy the cheap rents and the atmosphere of faded glories. Today it is a socially mixed area once more but there are still many older residents clinging to their habitual ways.

San Telmo is now a major tourist attraction. The heart of the *barrio* is the Plaza Dorrego, a small square surrounded by antique shops, art studios, bric-a-brac shops, cafés, bars and nightclubs. Every Sunday there is a flea market in the Plaza where Argentines of all ages love to wander around the stalls looking at the antiques, junk, handicrafts and jewellery on offer. Well worth a visit.

10

La Boca

The most colourful working class neighbourhood of Buenos Aires is La Boca. It lies by the Riochuelo Canal, south of the city centre near San Telmo and was originally established by French Basques, Andalusians from Spain and southern Italian families. The Italian stevedores, meatpackers and warehousemen and their families brightened up their tiny houses, often constructed using tin and metal sheeting scavenged from ships, by painting them with the pastel shades and bright colours of their native southern Italy. It is still largely a working class area though some Bohemian artists still have their workplaces there, following the great Argentine artist Benito Quinquela Martín who captured the spirit of the *barrio* so vividly in his great murals and artworks before the Second World War.

The best place to start in La Boca is a small street, almost an alleyway, called Caminito where Quinquela Martín established his base and which is still the centre for today's artists in residence. The area is a delight of cobbled streets shaded by sycamore trees, but beware of getting too close to the old Riochuelo waterways - it can still give off some pretty obnoxious odours, specially in the summertime.

The Tango

San Telmo is the heartland of the Tango, the slow but intensely passionate dance which Argentina gave to the world between the two World Wars. It is not unusual on a Sunday in the Plaza to see street artists dressed in Twenties style performing the tango in the roadway for entertainment for the passers by. The area is studded with Tango Bars, particularly on and around Balcarca Street where you can listen to tango music or be entertained by local residents enjoying the dance themselves or watching professional tango artists perform.

If you are there in the evening, head for Calle Necochea. This street still has rather garish dancehalls, nightclubs, pizzerias and bars which are not anywhere near as dangerous as they look but still retain some of the old reckless spirit and spontanaiety of the age when the tango was king and when the area was famed for its speakeasy bars and houses of ill repute. One word of caution - do not say anything, even in jest, against their beloved football team, Boca Juniors, or their greatest local footballing hero, Diego Maradona!

Sightseeing outside Buenos Aires

Buenos Aires covers an immense area. It takes hours just to cross the city by road. Getting to see anything beyond the city therefore involves a minimum of a day. Luján is accessible in a long day and Montevideo can also be done by air in a day but for the other places recommended in this section, a minimum stay of one night is necessary, and preferably two.

The Iguazú Falls

There are many regular flights from Buenos Aires to Puerta Iguazú or to Posadas airport where frequent buses will take you on to Puerto Iguazú. Really the best way of arranging this is a package deal through a Buenos Aires

10

travel agent. There are plentiful and relatively inexpensive all-in trips on offer in almost every agency. They will also offer you a trip to stay on the Brazilian side of the Falls if you prefer. The Iguazú Falls are among the world's most spectacular waterfalls and cataracts on the Iguazú River which marks the border between Brazil and Argentina, not far from the Paraguayan border further upstream. Nearly 2 million litres of water pass through and over the cataracts and waterfalls every second!

The best views of the Falls are generally agreed to be from the Brazilian side of the river. Crossing by ferry is cheap and easy but don't forget your passport! It is also a chance to sample the excellent Brazilian food. You can get right up to the Falls – even get soaked in the spray if you wish, so make sure you have shoes with a good grip and that you aren't wearing or carrying anything you don't want to get wet!

The area has many good hotels of all standards but usually you will have one selected for your package deal. If not, the International Iguazú is well situated near the Falls and has a swimming pool and fine restaurant.

10

Mar del Plata

If a stay at the beach is more your idea of relaxation then Mar del Plata is within easy reach of Buenos Aires. Though it is only 400 kms. from the capital the five-hour journey by road can be dangerously full of traffic, so your best bet is by air or a much less comfortable rail journey. There are frequent flights from Jorge Newberry airport which take about 40-45 minutes. Trains go from Constitución Station and take over four hours. Again, travel agents offer a wide range of package deals, but be sure to ask closely about hotel location and standards. Try and get near the Playa Grande, which is the best of the beaches in the resort.

Montevideo

Uruguay is the smallest country in South America and has a total population of some three million people. The Uruguayan capital, home to about one and a half million citizens, lies opposite Buenos Aires on the other side of the river Plate estuary. It is only one-tenth the size of Buenos Aires and in some ways resembles a slower, sleepier version of its neighbours. There is the feeling of a city which has seen better times but the Uruguayans are a friendly and welcoming people who will try and make your stay enjoyable. There are some interesting residential areas downtown but the architecture is so similar to some parts of Buenos Aires that is not worth visiting for that purpose alone. With no particular tourist sites in the city, most visitors simply wander around the older area between the Plaza Independencia and the port.

You can also spend the day on one of the very attractive beaches. Pocitos is elegant, though to see the best of the Uruguayan beach resorts you will need to travel a further 135 km. by bus along the coast to Punta del Este. This resort has become extremely popular with Argentines fleeing the oppressive heat of Buenos Aires summer who choose here as much as they also use Mar del Plata in their own country. You will also find the nightlife sparse after what is on offer from its big sister capital! Food is the same standard and type as in Buenos Aires.

There are regular flights from Jorge Newberry airport and there are also ferry connections. Be aware though that the airport in Montevideo is a half hour bus ride outside the city. If you have a lot of time to spare you can go by bus for around ten and a half hours or take a ferry (ten hours). If you are in more of a hurry, then try the hydrofoil connection across the river. Again, package deals are on offer but if you prefer to organise visits yourself, the Victoria Plaza Hotel on the Plaza Independencia is one of the best in the downtown area.

Luján

Nearly 70 kms. from Buenos Aires, Luján marks the place where the Argentine faithful believe a statue of the Virgin Mary, in transit to elsewhere in Argentina, insisted on taking up residence. It can be reached by train from Once Station or by bus from Plaza Miserere or Plaza Italia. Your hotel can arrange tickets. A day trip is sufficient to see the sights.

A shrine was built to house the statue, and the Virgin of Luján is now the patron saint of Argentina. The shrine, about five kilometres outside the town, has now become a basilica and place of pilgrimage for the faithful and those seeking favours or cures from the Virgin. If you like Catholic pilgrimages sites and have been to Fatima in

Portugal or Lourdes in France then you will know more or less what to expect. Luján also boasts an interesting Colonial and Historical Museum dedicated to the history of the area and housing a wide-ranging collection of artefacts dating from pre-Colonial times.

Tigre

Just north of the capital, and easily accessible by rail, is Tigre, a town nestling amongst the waterways of the Rio Paraná delta. It can be comfortably reached by local train from Retiro station or by bus. The journey is slow, taking around ninety minutes. Tickets can be bought at the station or through travel agents for a day tour. Once there, if you have not bought a package, take a guided tour for around $30 or try using the collective launches which will ferry you in and out of the maze of waterways and drop you off or pick you up like a water taxi. They are cheap and frequent, by far the best way to explore the delta. If you are sensitive to insects bites be sure you take defensive measures - with so much water, humidity and vegetation around the local insects thrive and their bite only begins to hurt when they put you down! Best ask in your hotel when this is likely to be a problem.

10

At the heart of the area is Isla Martín García which is strategically placed in the delta and as such has been the scene of several important military events in Argentine history. It has several historical buildings of interest and a relaxingly pleasant nature reserve. The cluster of islands, lush vegetation, crumbling old houses and modern holiday residences make a refreshing change of atmosphere from downtown Buenos Aires.

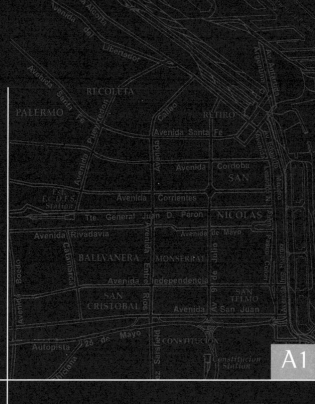

Appendix one

appendix one

Some useful addresses and contact details.

Embassies

Australian Embassy
Villanueva 1400, Palermo
Buenos Aires
❏ Tel: (11) 4777 6580

Brazilian Embassy
Av. Belgrano 1670, 1st. Floor
Montserrat
Buenos Aires
❏ Tel: (11) 4381 0539

British Embassy
Dr. Luis Agote 2412
1425 Buenos Aires
❏ Tel: (11) 4803 7070/4803 779; fax: 4806 5713

Argentine-British Chamber of Commerce
25 de Mayo 586
Buenos Aires
❏ Tel: (11) 4394 2872/2318/2762; fax: 4394 2282

Canadian Embassy
Tagle 2828, Palermo
Buenos Aires
❏ Tel: (11) 4805 3032

Chilean Embassy
San Martín 439, 9th Floor
San Nicolás
Buenos Aires
❏ Tel: (11) 4394 6582

French Embassy
Santa Fé 846, 3rd Floor
Retiro
Buenos Aires
❏ Tel: (11) 4312 2409

German Embassy
Villanueva 1055, Palermo
Buenos Aires
❏ Tel: (11) 4778 2500

Greek Embassy
Av. Roque Saenz Peña 547, 4th Floor
Buenos Aires
❏ Tel: (11) 4342 4958/0528

A1

Irish Embassy
Suipacha 1380, Retiro
Buenos Aires
❏ Tel: (11) 4325 8588

Israeli Embassy
Av. De Mayo 701, 10th Floor
Montserrat
Buenos Aires
❏ Tel: (11) 4342 6932/1465/1797

Italian Embassy
Av. Marcelo T. Alvear 1149
Retiro
Buenos Aires
❏ Tel: (11) 4816 6132

Japanese Embassy
Bouchard 547, 15th Floor
San Nicolás
Buenos Aires
❏ Tel: (11) 4318 8220

Netherlands Embassy
Avenida de Mayo 701, 19th Floor
Montserrat
Buenos Aires
❏ Tel: (11) 4334 4000

New Zealand Embassy
Av. Corrientes 456, 6th Floor
Buenos Aires
❏ Tel: (11) 4328 0747

South African Embassy
Av. Marcelo T. Alvear 590, 8th Floor
Buenos Aires
❏ Tel: (11)4317 2900

Swiss Embassy
Santa Fé 846, 10th Floor
Retiro
Buenos Aires
❏ Tel: (11) 4311 6491

Uruguayan Embassy
Las Heras 1907
Recoleta
Buenos Aires
❏ Tel: (11) 4807 3040

A1

U.S.Embassy
Colombia 4300, Palermo
Buenos Aires
❑ Tel: (11) 4774 4533/4

Diplomatic Representation Abroad
Australia
Trade Office in Sydney
1/13 Alfred St
Sydney, NSW 2000
❑ Tel: +61 (2) 9251 3402/3; fax: +61 (2) 9251 340

Belgium
Embassy in Belgium
Avenue Louise 225, B.P. 6
1050 Brussels, Belgium
❑ Tel: +32 (2) 647 7812, 647 9002, 647 9319, 649 0380
(Trade Office); fax: +32 (2) 647 9319, 642 9187 (Trade
Office)

Canada
Embassy in Canada
90 Sparks St., Suite 910
Ottawa, ON KIP 5B4
❑ Tel: +1 (613) 236 2351/4; fax: +1 (613) 235 2659

Denmark
Trade Ofiice in Copenhagen
Kastelsvej 15, 1st Fl.
2100 Copenhagen
❑ Tel: +45 3315 8082/9526, 3312 5211;
fax: +45 3315 5574

Egypt
Trade Office in Cairo
17 Brasil St., 8th Fl., Apt. 51
PO Box 247
Dokki Zamalek
Cairo
❑Tel +20 (2) 340 9241; fax: +20 (2) 340 8652

France
Embassy in France
6 Rue Cimarosa
75116 Paris
❑Tel: +33 (1) 45 53 33 00, 4405 2700/40
fax: +33 (1) 45 53 46 33

A1

Germany
Argentine Promotion Centre
W. Frankfurt
Mainzer Landstrasse Y6, 14th Floor
60325 Frankfurt/Main
❑Tel: +46 69 0720030, 97200311; fax: +49 69 175419

Greece
Embassy in Greece
59 Leof Vassilissis Sophia
Athens 140
❑Tel: +30 (1) 72 24 753, 72 24 710, 72 24 158
fax: +30 (1) 72 27 568

Japan
Embassy in Japan
120 1 Moto Azabu 2 chome
Minato ku
Tokyo
❑Tel: +81 (3) 5420 7101/5

Netherlands
Embassy in the Netherlands
Javastraat 20
The Hague

New Zealand
Embassy in New Zealand
75 Homebrush Rd., Khadalla, Lamb
Quay P.O. Box 5430
Wellington, New Zealand
❑Tel: +64 (4) 479 7445; fax: +64 (4) 479 7344

Norway
Embassy in Norway
Drammensreien 39
0244 Oslo
❑Tel: +47 22 55 24 48/9; fax: +47 22 44 16 41

Saudi Arabia
Embassy in Saudi Arabia
Olaya Building P.5 Of. 503
PO Box 94369
Riyadh 11693
❑Tel: +966 (1) 465 2600, 465 6064
fax: +966 (1) 465 3057

A1

South Africa
Embassy in South Africa
200 Standard Plaza
0002 Pretoria, Rep. of South Africa
❑Tel: +27 (12) 433 527, 433 516
fax: +27 (12) 433 521

Spain
Embassy in Spain
Calle Pedro de Valdivia 21
28046 Madrid
❑Tel: +34 (1) 562 2800; fax: +34 (1) 563 5185

Consulate General in Barcelona
Paseo de la Gracia 11 B, Piso 2
Barcelona 08007
❑Tel: +34 (3) 3412 7949, 317 4149/3058

Consulate General in Las Palmas
Av. Franchi No. 5, Piso 2, Of. 10 y 12
Las Palmas
❑Tel: +34 (28) 26 1418, 27 6558

Consulate General in Madrid
Ortega y Gasset 62
Madrid 28006
❑Tel: +34 (1) 402 5115, 402 5248
fax: +34 (1) 309 1996

Consulate General in Vigo
Marques de Valladares 5, Piso 3
Apdo. Postal 1520
36201 Vigo, Pontevedra
❑Tel: +34 (86) 43 5822, 43 9292; fax: +34 (86) 43 9292

Sweden
Embassy in Sween
Grevgatan 5 2nd floor
PO Box 14039
10440 Stockholm, Sweden
❑Tel: +46 (8) 663 19 65; fax: +46 (8) 661 0009

Switzerland
Embassy in Switzerland
Jungfraustrasse 1
3005 Berne
❑Tel: +41 (31) 352 3565/6, 443 3566/7
fax: +41 (31) 352 1519

A1

Taiwan
Commercial Office in Taiwan
International Trade Building, Suite 1003
333 Keelung Road, Sec. 1
Taipei, Taiwan
❑Tel: +886 (2) 758 9433; fax:+886 (2) 758 9423

Turkey
Embassy in Turkey
Ugur Mumcu Cadderi 60/3
06700 Gaxiosman pase
Cankaya, Ankara
❑Tel: [90] (312) 446 2061/2

United Kingdom
Embassy in the United Kingdom
65 Brook Street
London W1Y0 1YE
❑Tel: +44 (171) 318 1300/1330/1328

United States of America
Embassy in the United States of America
1600 New Hampshire Avenue NW
Washington, DC 20009
❑Tel: +1 (202) 939 6400, 939 6431, 939 6416
fax: +1 (202) 332 3171

Office of the Argentine Financial Representative
1901 L St., NW, Suite 606
Washington DC 20036
❑Tel: +1 (202) 466 3021; fax: +1 (202) 463 8793

Consulate General and Trade Office in Atlanta
245 Peachtree Ctr. Ave. Suite 2101
Atlanta GA 30303
❑Tel: +1 (404) 880 0805; fax: +1 (404) 880 0806

Consulate and Trade Office in Chicago
205 N. Michigan Ave., Suite 4208/9
Chicago, IL 60601
❑Tel: 1 (312) 819 2620, 819 2610 (Trade Office)
fax: +1 (312) 819 2626, 819 2612 (Trade Office)

Consulate and Trade Office in Houston
1990 Post Oak Blvd., Suite 770
Houston, TX 77056
❑Tel: +1 (713) 871 8935; fax: +1 (713) 871 0639

A1

Consulate and Trade Office in Los Angeles
5055 Wilshire Blvd. Suite 210
Los Angeles, CA 90036
❏Tel: +1 (213) 954 9155, 954 9233
fax: +1 (213) 937 3874, 937 3841

Consulate and Trade Office in Miami
800 Brickell Avenue, Penthouse 1
Miami, FL 33131
❏Tel: +1 (305) 373 7794; fax: +1 (305) 371 7108

Consulate General in New York
12 West 56th St.
New York, NY 10019
❏Tel: +1 (212) 603 0400/0403/0410
fax: +1 (212) 541 7746

Airlines

Aerolineas Argentinas
Perú 2
❏ Tel: (11) 4340 7777

Air France
Paraguay 610, 14th Floor
❏ Tel: (11) 4317 4747

Alitalia
Suipacha 1111 28th Floor
❏ Tel: (11) 4310 9910

American Airlines
Av. Santa Fé 81
❏ Tel: (11) 4318 1111

Austral
Paraná 590 and San Martín 427
❏ Tel: (11) 4340 7777

Avianca
Carlos Pellegrini 1163, 4th Floor
❏ Tel: (11) 4322 2731

British Airways
Víamonte 570
❏ Tel: (11) 4320 6600

Canadian Airlines
Av. Córdoba 656
❏ Tel: (11) 4322 3632

A1

Iberia
Carlos Pellegrini 1163, 1st Floor
❏ Tel: (11) 4326 5082

KLM
Reconquista 559, 5th Floor
❏ Tel: (11) 4312 1200/2660

LADE
Per˙ 714
❏ Tel: (11) 4361 0853

LAPA
Carlos Pellegrini 1075
❏ Tel: (11) 4819 5272

Lufthansa
Av. Marcelo T. Alvear 636
❏ Tel: (11) 4319 0600

Pluna
Florida 1
❏ Tel: (11) 4342 7000

South African Airways
Av. Santa Fé 794, 3rd Floor
❏ Tel: (11) 4311 8184

Swissair
Av. Santa Fé 846, 1st Floor
❏ Tel: (11) 4319 0000

Transbrasil
Florida 780, 1st Floor
❏ Tel: (11) 4394 8424

United Airlines
Av. Madero 900, 9th Floor
Torre Catalinas Plaza
❏ Tel: (11) 4316 0777

VARIG
Carabelas 344
❏ Tel: (11) 4329 9211

VASP
Av. Santa Fé 784
Tel: (11) 4312 8520

A1

Railways
Retiro Station
Av. Ramos Mejía
❑ Tel: (11) 4311 8704/8264

Constitución Station
General Hornos 11
❑ Tel: (11) 4304 0028/31

Once Station
Avenidas Pueyrredón and Bartelomeo Mitre
❑ Tel: (11) 4861 0043

Bus Services
Manuel Tienda Leon (Airport to Downtown buses)
Av. Santa Fé 790
❑ Tel: (11) 4315 0489/4311 3722

San Martín Bus (Airport to downtown buses)
Av. Santa Fé 887
❑ Tel: (11) 4314 4747/4480 9464

Estación Terminal Retiro (Buses to Provinces etc.)
Retiro
❑ Tel: (11) 4310 0700

Ferries
Buquebus
Av. Córdoba and Eduardo Madero
❑ Tel: 4316 6500/6550

Cacciola S.A.
Florida 520, 1st. Floor
❑ Tel: 4393 6100

Ferrytur
Av. Córdoba 699
❑ Tel: 4315 6800

Tourist Information
Secretaría de Turismo de la Nación
Av. Santa Fé 883
❑ Tel: 4312 2232/5550
Opens: 0900 - 1700. Closed weekends.

A1

Aeropuerto Internacional de Ezeiza
Open 0900 - 2000, Saturdays 0900 - 1400. Closed
Sundays

Aeroparque Jorge Newberry
Open 0900 - 2000, Saturdays 0900 - 1400. Closed
Sundays

Dirección General de Turismo de Buenos Aires
Centro Cultural Genral San Martín
Sarmiento 1551, 4th Floor
❑ Tel: (11) 4372 3612
Open 0900 - 1700, Saturdays 0900 - 1400. Closed
Sundays

Florida and Diagonal Roque Saenz Peña
Open 0900 - 2000, Saturdays 0900 - 1400. Closed
Sundays

Galerias Pacifico: Florida and Av. Córdoba
Open 0900 - 1400, Saturdays 0900 - 1400. Closed
Sundays
For Guided Tours of the city: ❑ Tel: 4372 3612

A1

Car Hire
Alamo
Florida 375 Piso 2
Buenos Aires
❑ Tel: (11) 4325 7000

Budget
Viamonte 611 Piso 11
Buenos Aires
❑ Tel: (11) 4322 8409

Dollar
Av. Marcelo T. Alvear 523
Buenos Aires
❑ Tel: (11) 4315 8800

Hertz
Ricardo Rojas 451
Buenos Aires
❑ Tel: (11) 4312 1317

Thrifty
Av. Leandro N. Alem 699
Buenos Aires
❑ Tel: (11) 4315 0777

appendix two

appendix two

The Spanish Language

Argentines appreciate foreigners trying to speak their language and are tolerant of mistakes in grammar and pronunciation. If you know no Spanish at all just use the third column in this vocabulary as a guide to pronunciation.

You will find Argentine Spanish differs markedly from the Spanish spoken in Spain or most of the rest of South America. The Italian influence on pronunciation, slang and vocabulary is very strong, especially in Buenos Aires where around one in three citizens is of Italian origin. Don't be afraid to have a go at pronouncing words in the *porteño* way, but bear in mind that any Italian-sounding vocabulary you pick up in Buenos Aires may sound odd to the ears of other Latin Americans living outside Argentina and Uruguay.

Pronunciation is not difficult if you bear these basics in mind:

Vowels are standard:

a	as in hat
e	as in met
i	as in fee
o	as in hot
u	as in the 'oo' of boot
y	when used alone means 'and', and in Spain is pronounced as 'ee' in 'fee'. Beside a vowel it is pronounced as a 'I' – eg. *Ayer* (yesterday) = *I-air*. In Argentina 'y' is generally pronounced in the same way as **ll**, i.e. more like 'sz' - a combination of the j of 'jest' and the z of 'zest'.

Most consonants are similar to English except:

c	usually pronounced as a hard k except when used before 'i' or 'e' when it is pronounced 's'.
d	as in English at the beginning of a word, but silent at the end of a word. E.g. *Salud* (cheers!)= *sal-oo*.
g	normally hard as in 'God' but before 'e' or 'i' is soft as the 'ch' of Loch Lomond. E.g. *Gente* (people) = *hen-tay* .
h	always silent. E.g. *Hombre* (man) = *om-bray*. When combined with a 'c' (**ch**) it is pronounced

A2

as in English. E.g. *mucho* (much) = *moo-cho*.

j   as 'h' in 'hello'. E.g. *fijo* (fig) = *fee-hoh*

ll   when two 'l's are found together they become 'y' . E.g. *Calle* (street) = *ca-yeh*. Only in Argentina and Uruguay is this notably converted into more of an 'sz' sound and becomes *casz-yeh*, more like the combination of the j of 'jest' and the z of 'zest' There is no equivalent in English.

ñ   When 'n' has an accent (tilda) above it, it is pronounced *neen-yoh*, as in 'opinion'.

qu   always a hard 'k'. E.g. *Queso* (cheese) = *keh-soh*

rr   as in English but trilled, i e. dwelling on the letter and repeating it rapidly. E.g *Cerrito* = *serrrr-ee-toh*

x   Normally as in 'taxi' but can be pronounced as the 'ch' of 'loch' E.g. *Xavier* is = *Have-ee-air*.

z   more like the 's' of 'see'. E.g. *Brazo* (arm) = *brass-oh*.

The very strongly Italianate Spanish spoken in Buenos Aires and throughout Argentina in general has certain key features. Known as *lunfardo* it has colloquialisms you would be very unwise to attempt unless you are absolutely sure of its nuances. In showing off your limited local knowledge of language and pronunciation you may give unwitting offence, so avoid the temptation!

Common *lunfardo* words you may hear include:

guita   money (**gwee-tah**)

morfar   to eat (**mor-far**) – a corruption of Peninsula Spanish.

macanudo   fine; great; really good! (**mack-an-oo-doh**) Not a reference to a lost Scottish clan in Patagonia.

pibe   kid, young chap (**pee-beh**). Can be either affectionate or pejorative. Used often about footballers.

pucho   cigarette (**pooh-choh**)

You also need to be aware of a couple of false friends where the Spanish word resembles an English word but has a distinctly different meaning. For example:

A2

molestar   does not mean to molest someone! It
means to bother or annoy

bárbaro   means brilliant or really good, not
barbarous or barbaric

embarazada means pregnant not embarassed

introducir means to insert – not to be used when
introducing someone! If in doubt, take the
safe option – use English !

Punctuation

In written Spanish, exclamations and questions are
marked by an inverted exclamation or question mark at
the beginning of the sentence, as well as the normal
marks at the end of the sentence. E.g.*¿Habla usted
Inglés?* ('Do you speak English?)

Useful Vocabulary

Emergency Vocabulary

police	*policía*	poll-iss-ee-ah
call the police	*llame la policía*	ya-may la-poll-iss-ee-ah
danger	*peligro*	pell-ee-groh
doctor	*médico*	meh-dee-ko
call a doctor	*llame un médico*	ya-may oon med-ee-ko
fire	*fuego*	fway-go
look out!	*¡cuidado!*	kwee-da-doh
help me!	*¡ayúdarme!*	a-yoo-da-meh

Numbers

one	*uno/a*	oo-no, oonah
two	*dos*	doss
three	*tres*	tress
four	*cuatro*	kwa-troh
five	*cinco*	sin-koh
six	*seis*	sey-ss

A2

seven	*siete*	see-eh-teh
eight	*ocho*	otch-oh
nine	*nueve*	nweh-veh
ten	*diez*	dee-ess
eleven	*once*	on-say
twelve	*doce*	doss-say
thirteen	*trece*	tress-say
fourteen	*catorce*	cat-orse-say
fifteen	*quince*	keen-say
sixteen	*dieciséis*	dee-ess-ee-says
seventeen	*diecisiete*	dee-ess-ee-seh-tay
eighteen	*dieciocho*	dee-ess-ee-otcho
nineteen	*diecinueve*	dee-ess-ee-nweh-veh
twenty	*veinte*	beyn-teh
twenty-one	*veinte uno*	beyn-teh oo-no
thirty	*treinta*	train-tah
forty	*cuarenta*	kwa-rent-ah
fifty	*cincuenta*	sin-kwen-tah
sixty	*sesenta*	sess-en-tah
seventy	*setenta*	set-en-tah
eighty	*ochenta*	otch-en-tah
ninety	*noventa*	nov-en-tah
hundred	*cien*	see-en
thousand	*mil*	meel
million	*millon*	me-yon

Time

today	*hoy*	oy
tomorrow	*mañana*	ma-nya-nah
yesterday	*ayer*	I-yair
day	*día*	dee-ah

weekend	*fín de semana*	**fin de sem-ah-nah**
Monday	*lunes*	**loo-ness**
Tuesday	*martes*	**mar-tess**
Wednesday	*miércoles*	**mee-erk-ko-less**
Thursday	*jueves*	**huay-ves**
Friday	*viernes*	**vee-er-ness**
Saturday	*sábado*	**sa-ba-doh**
Sunday	*domingo*	**doh-min-go**
week	*semana*	**se-ma-nah**
month	*mes*	**mess**
January	*enero*	**eh-nair-oh**
February	*febrero*	**feb-rare-oh**
March	*marzo*	**mar-so**
April	*abril*	**a-breel**
May	*mayo*	**my-oh**
June	*junio*	**hoo-nee-oh**
July	julio	**hoo-lee-oh**
August	*agosto*	**agg-ost-oh**
September	*septiembre*	**sept-ee-em-bray**
October	*octubre*	**oct-oo-bray**
November	*noviembre*	**no-vem-bray**
December	*diciembre*	**dee-see-em-bray**
year	*año*	**an-yoh**
first	*primero*	**pree-mare-oh**
second	*segundo*	**seg-oon-doh**
third	*tercero*	**terr-sair-oh**

A2

A2

Everyday Words

yes	*sí*	see
no	*no*	noh
Sir	*Señor*	sen-yorr
Madam	*Señora*	sen-yorr-ah
Miss	*Señorita*	sen-yorr-ee-tah
please	*por favor*	pour fah-vorr
thank you	*gracias*	grass-ee-ass
hello	*hola*	o-lah
help me!	*ayudame*	ah-yoo-dah-may
important	*importante*	imp-ort-ant-eyh
urgent	*urgente*	oor-hen-tay
good	*bueno*	bweno
bad	*malo*	ma-loh
goodbye	*adiós*	add-ee-oss
good morning	*buenos días*	bwenos dee-ass
good afternoon	*buenas tardes*	bwenas tar-days
good evening	*buenas tardes*	bwenas tar-days
excuse me	*perdón*	per-don
where is?	*¿dónde está?*	don-day-estah
what is?	*¿qué es?*	kay-ess
who is?	*¿quién es?*	kyen-ess
how much?	*¿cuánto?*	kwahn-toh
how many ?	*¿cuántos?*	kwahn-toss
do you speak English?	*¿habla usted Inglés ?*	ablah-oostedd-in-glaze
I do not speak Spanish	*no hablo español*	no-abloh-es-pan-yoll
I don't understand	*no comprendo*	no-com-prend-oh
do you understand?	*¿comprende usted?*	com-prend-eh-oostedd

I want	*yo quiero*	**yo kee-air-oh**
I'm lost	*estoy perdido*	**es-toy-perd-eed-oh**
I'm looking for	*estoy buscando*	**es-toy buss-can-doh**
can I?/may I?	*¿puedo?*	**pweyh-doh**
can I have?	*¿puede darme?*	**pway-day-dar-may**
I have	*tengo*	**ten-goh**
I don't have	*no tengo*	**no ten-goh**
I'm hungry	*tengo hambre*	**ten-goh-am-bray**
I'm thirsty	*tengo sed*	**ten-goh-sedd**
There is/are	*hay*	**eye**
There isn't/aren't	*no hay*	**no eye**
a little	*un-poco*	**un-poke-oh**
a lot	*mucho*	**moo-choh**
too much	*demasiado*	**de-mass-eeh-ah-doh**
hot	*caliente*	**kall-eeh-ent-eh**
cold	*frío*	**free-oh**
the next	*el próximo*	**el-prox-eeh-mohw**
near	*cerca*	**serr-kah**
until	*hasta*	**ass-tah**
now	*ahora*	**ah-or-ah**
soon	*pronto*	**pron-toh**
perhaps	*tal vez*	**tahll-vess**

Travelling

taxi	*taxi*	**taxi**
bus	*bus*	**booss**
bus station	*estación de bus*	**ess-tass-eeh-on-de booss**
aeroplane	*avión*	**av-eeh-on**

A2

A2

airport	*aeropuerto*	air-oh-pwer-toh
train	*tren*	trenn
train station	*estación de ferrocarril*	ess-tass-eeh-on de-ferro-carrr-eel
take me to	*lléveme a*	yeh-veh-may-ah
stop here please	*pare aquí por favor*	pa-ray-ah-kee pour-fav-or

Eating out, Food and Drink

breakfast	*desayuno*	dess-ah-yoo-no
lunch	*almuerzo*	al-mwer-so
dinner	*cena*	sen-ah
snack	*merienda*	merry-end-ah
restaurant	*restaurante*	rest-orr-ant-ay
the menu	*la carta*	la-cart-ah
plate	*plato*	plat-oh
glass	*vaso*	vass-oh
cup	*taza*	tass-ah
knife	*cuchillo*	coo-chee-oh
fork	*tenedor*	ten-eh-door
spoon	*cuchara*	coo-char-ah
napkin	*servilleta*	ser-vee-ett-ah
ashtray	*cenicero*	sen-ee-ser-oh
waiter	*Mesero/Señor*	mess-air-oh/sen-yorr
waitress	*Señora/Señorita*	sen-yorr-ah sen-yorr-ee-tah
more	*más*	mass
no more	*no más*	no mass
enough	*suficiente*	soo-fiss-ee-ent-ay
less	*menos*	may-noss
with	*con*	con

the bill	*la cuenta*	**la-kwen-tah**
food	*comida*	**com-ee-dah**
drink	*bebida*	**beb-ee-dah**
starter	*entrada*	**en-tra-dah**
main course	*plato principal*	**plat-oh preen-see-pal**
dessert	*postre*	**poss-tray**
water	*agua*	**ag-wah**
mineral water	*agua mineral*	**ag-wah mee-neral**
soda water	*agua con gas*	**ag-wah con gas**
aperitif	*aperitivo*	**aperit-eev-oh**
a bottle	*una botella*	**oonah bot-eyah**
half a bottle	*media botella*	**med-ee-ah bot-eyah**
red wine	*vino tinto*	**vee-no tin-toh**
white wine	*vino blanco*	**vee-no blank-oh**
dry	*seco*	**sekko**
sweet	*dulce*	**dool-say**
beer	*cerveza*	**ser-vay-sah**
juice	*jugo*	**who-go**
tea	*té*	**teh**
coffee	*café*	**kaff-eh**
sugar	*azucar*	**ah-zoo-kah**
milk	*leche*	**letch-eh**
bread	*pan*	**pan**
toast	*pan tostado*	**pan tossed-adoh**
butter	*mantequilla*	**man-teh-kee-yah**
salt	*sal*	**sal**
pepper	*pimienta*	**pim-ee-ent-ah**
soup	*sopa*	**sopp-ah**
salad	*ensalada*	**en-sah-lah-dah**

A2

oil	*aceite*	ass-ay-teh
vineger	*vinagre*	vin-ag-ray
meat	*carne*	car-neh
steak	*bife*	bee-fay
fillet	*lomo*	low-mow
fish	*pescado*	pess-cah-doh
seafood	*mariscos*	mar-ees-kohs
pork	*cerdo*	ser-doh
lamb	*cordero*	cord-air-oh
veal	*ternera*	turn-air-oh
chicken	*pollo*	poyh-oh
sausages	*chorizo*	chore-ee-soh
ham	*jamón*	ham-on
potatoes	*papas /patatas*	pap-ahs / patatas
rice	*arroz*	arr-oz
pasta	*pasta*	past-ah
vegetables	*verduras*	ver-dure-ahs
eggs	*huevos*	way-vohs
cheese	*queso*	kay-soh
grilled	*a la parilla*	a la parrr-ee-yah
fried	*frita*	free-tah
baked	*al horno*	al-orr-no
boiled	*cocido*	koh-seed-oh
smoked	*ahumado*	ah-oo-mah-doh
poached	*hervido*	her-vee-doh
stew	*estofado*	ess-tow-fa-doh
barbecued	*barbacoa/ a la leña*	bar-ba-ko-ah a la len-yah
uncooked	*crudo*	crew-doh
in pastry	*empanada*	em-pan-ah-dah
in a sauce	*en salsa*	en-sal-sah

A2

tart	*tarta*	**tarta**
cake	*pastel*	**pass-tell**
icecream	*helado*	**hell-ah-doh**
flan	*flan*	**flan**
fruit	*fruta*	**froo-tah**

Shopping

Where is the...?	*¿donde está la..?*	**don-day ess-tah la**
chemist	*farmacia*	**farm-ass-ee-ah**
stationers	*papelería*	**pap-ell-err-ee-ah**
bookshop	*librería*	**lib-rerr-ee-ah**
the market	*el mercado*	**el-merk-ah-doh**
souvenir shop	*tienda de regalos*	**tee-end-ah de reg-ah-lows**
dry cleaners	*tintorería*	**tin-tor-er-ee-ah**
hairdressers	*peluquería*	**pell-ook-er-ee-ah**
news stand	*quiosco*	**kee-oss-ko**
I want to buy	*quiero comprar*	**kyeer-oh com-pra**
how much?	*¿cuánto vale?*	**kwan-toh-val-eh**
it's too much	*es demasiado*	**es de-mass-ee-ahd-oh**
I don't like it	*no me gusta*	**no-meh-goo-stah**
I'll take it	*me le llevo*	**meh-loh-yay-vo**
thank you	*gracias*	**grass-ee-ass**
no thanks	*no gracias*	**no grass-ee-ass**
cheap	*barato*	**bah-rat-oh**
cheaper	*mas barato*	**mass-bah-rat-oh**
entrance	*entrada*	**en-tra-dah**
exit	*salida*	**sal-ee-dah**

Money

| money | *dinero* | **dee-nair-oh** |
| bank | *banco* | **ban-koh** |

A2

175

Money Exchange	*casa de cambio*	**cassa-de-cam-bee-oh**
dollars	*dólares*	**doll-ar-ess**
pounds	*libras esterlinas*	**lee-bras-est-erl-een-as**
francs	*francos*	**fran-kos**
marks	*marcos*	**mar-kos**
lira	*liras*	**lee-rahs**
yen	*yen*	**yen**
I want to change	*quiero cambiar*	**kyeer-oh-cam-bee-ar**
What is the exchange rate for?	*¿a cómo está el cambio para..?*	**a-komo-ess-tah el-kam-bee-oh parra...?**
what is the commission rate?	*¿qué comisión cargan ?*	**kay-comm-iss-ee-on car-gan**
Business		
how are you?	*¿cómo está usted?*	**Komo-es-tah-oo-sted**
pleased to meet you	*mucho gusto*	**moo-cho-goo-stoh**
excuse me	*con permiso*	**con-per-mee-soh**
of course	*por supuesto*	**por-soo-pwess-toh**
it isn't important	*no importa*	**no-im-por-tah**
it is important	*es importante*	**es-im-port-anteh**
how do you say?	*¿cómo se dice?*	**ko-mo-se-dee-say**
why?	*¿por qué?*	**por-kay**
when?	*¿cuándo?*	**kwan-doh**
how Many ?	*¿cuántos?*	**kwan-tos**
who?	*¿quién?*	**kee-en**
because	*por qué*	**por-kay**
accountant	*contador*	**kon-tad-or**

A2

accounts	*contabilidad*	**kon-tah-billi-dad**
advertising	*publicidad*	**poo-bliss-ee-dad**
agency	*agencia*	**ah-hen-see-ah**
appointment	*cita*	**see-tah**
buyers	*compradores*	**kom-pra-dor-es**
sellers	*vendedores*	**ven-deh-dor-es**
bank loan	*préstamo*	**press-ta-moh**
boss	*jefe*	**heff-eh**
business	*negocio*	**neh-go-see-oh**
capital	*capital*	**ka-pee-tal**
chairman	*presidente*	**prez-ee-dent-eh**
charges	*cargos*	**kar-gos**
costs	*gastos*	**gas-toss**
collection (money)	*cobrar*	**ko-brar**
company	*compañía*	**kom-pan-ee-ah**
company (firm)	*empresa*	**em-press-ah**
contract	*contrato*	**kon-trat-oh**
credit	*crédito*	**kreh-dit-oh**
customer	*cliente*	**klee-en-teh**
deadline	*plazo límite*	**plazo-lee-mit-eh**
delivery	*entrega*	**en-tray-gah**
director	*director*	**dee-rect-or**
discount	*descuento*	**des-kwen-toh**
distributor	*distribuidor*	**dis-trib-wee-dor**
freight (costs)	*flete*	**fleh-teh**
guarantee	*garantía*	**gar-ant-ee-ah**
insurance	*seguro*	**seh-goo-roh**
interest	*interés*	**een-ter-ess**
investment	*inversión*	**een-ver-see-on**
invoice	*factura*	**fact-oo-rah**

A2

A2

invoicing	*facturación*	fact-oo-rah-see-on
job (position)	*puesto*	pwess-toh
lawyer	*abogado*	a-boh-gahd-oh
leaflet (brochure)	*folleto*	foy-et-oh
letter of credit	*carta de crédito*	kar-tah-de-cred-it-oh
license	*licencia*	lee-sen-see-ah
list	*lista*	lee-stah
manager	*gerente*	hair-ent-eh
offer (an)	*oferta*	off-err-ta
office	*oficina*	off-iss-ee-nah
packing	*embalaje*	em-bahl-ah-hey
patent	*patente*	pat-ent-eh
pay (to)	*pagar*	pag-ar
payment	*pago*	pa-go
price	*precio*	press-ee-oh
product	*producto*	proh-dook-toh
quality	*calidad*	kall-ee-dad
report	*informe*	in-form-eh
research	*investigación*	in-vest-ee-gas-tee-on
savings	*ahorros*	ah-orr-os
return (on investment)	*rendimiento*	ren-dee-mee-ent-oh
salary	*salario*	sal-are-ee-oh
samples	*muestras*	mwe-est-rah
sale (*n*)	*una venta*	oo-nah-ven-tah
sell (*v*)	*vender*	ven-dare
service	*servicio*	ser-viss-ee-oh
ship (to)	*enviar*	en-vee-ar
shipment	*envío*	en-vee-oh
shop	*tienda*	tee-end-ah

staff (employees)	*empleados*	**em-plee-ahd-os**
supplier	*proveedor*	**prov-eh-dor**
tarifs	*tarifas*	**tar-ee-fas**
taxes	*impuestos*	**imp-west-ohs**
trade mark	*marca registrada*	**markah-reg-is-trah-da**
to hire	*contratar*	**kon-trat-ah**
training	*capacitación*	**cap-ass-it-ass-ee-on**
until later	*hasta luego*	**ass-tah-lwey-go**
value	*valor*	**val-orr**
wage	*sueldo*	**swell-doh**
wholesaler	*mayorista*	**mah-yor-ees-tah**
work	*trabajo*	**trab-ah-ho**

A2

appendix three: commercial support for US companies

A3

appendix three

Directory of Export Assistance Centers

Cities in capital letters are centres which combine the export promotion and trade finance service of the Department of Commerce, the Export-Import Bank, the Small Business Administration and the Agency of International Development. (All numbers prefixed +1)

ALABAMA

Birmingham, Alabama - George Norton, Director
950 22nd Street North, Room 707, ZIP 35203
t: : (205) 731-1331   **f:** (205) 731-0076

ALASKA

Anchorage, Alaska - Charles Becker, Director
550 West 7th Ave., Suite 1770, ZIP: 99501
t: (907) 271-6237   **f:** (907) 271-6242

ARIZONA

A3

Phoenix, Arizona - Frank Woods, Director
2901 N. Central Ave., Suite 970, ZIP 85012
t: (602) 640-2513   **f:** (602) 640-2518

CALIFORNIA - LONG BEACH

Joseph F Sachs, Director
Mary Delmege, CS Director
One World Trade Center, Ste. 1670, ZIP: 90831
t: (562) 980-4550   **f:** (562) 980-4561

CALIFORNIA - SAN JOSE

101 Park Center Plaza, Ste. 1001, ZIP: 95113
t: (408) 271-7300   **f:** (408) 271-7307

COLORADO - DENVER

Nancy Charles-Parker, Director
1625 Broadway, Suite 680, ZIP: 80202
t: (303) 844-6623   **f:** (303) 844-5651

A3

CONNECTICUT
Middletown, Connecticut - Carl Jacobsen, Director
213 Court Street, Suite 903 ZIP: 06457-3346
t: (860) 638-6950   *f:* (860) 638-6970

DELAWARE
Served by the Philadelphia, Pennsylvania U.S. Export
 AssistanceCenter

FLORIDA - MIAMI
 John McCartney, Director
P.O. Box 590570, ZIP: 33159
5600 Northwest 36th St., Ste. 617, ZIP: 33166
t: (305) 526-7425   *f:* (305) 526-7434

GEORGIA - ATLANTA
Samuel Troy, Director
285 Peachtree Center Avenue, NE, Suite 200
ZIP: 30303-1229
t: (404) 657-1900   *f:* (404) 657-1970

HAWAII
Honolulu, Hawaii - Greg Wong, Manager
1001 Bishop St.; Pacific Tower; Suite 1140
ZIP: 96813
t: (808) 522-8040   *f:* (808) 522-8045

IDAHO
Boise, Idaho - James Hellwig, Manager
700 West State Street, 2nd Floor, ZIP: 83720
t: (208) 334-3857   *f:* (208) 334-2783

ILLINOIS - CHICAGO
 Mary Joyce, Director
55 West Monroe Street, Suite 2440, ZIP: 60603
t: (312) 353-8045   *f:* (312) 353-8120

INDIANA
Indianapolis, Indiana - Dan Swart, Manager
11405 N. Pennsylvania Street, Suite 106
Carmel, IN, ZIP: 46032
t: (317) 582-2300   *f:* (317) 582-2301

IOWA
Des Moines, Iowa - Allen Patch, Director
601 Locust Street, Suite 100, ZIP: 50309-3739
t: (515) 288-8614   *f:* (515) 288-1437

KANSAS
Wichita, Kansas - George D. Lavid, Manager
209 East William, Suite 300, ZIP: 67202-4001
t: (316) 269-6160   *f:* (316) 269-6111

KENTUCKY
Louisville, Kentucky - John Autin, Director
601 W. Broadway, Room 634B , ZIP: 40202
t: (502) 582-5066   *f:* (502) 582-6573

LOUISIANA - DELTA
Patricia Holt, Acting Director
365 Canal Street, Suite 1170
New Orleans ZIP: 70130
t: (504) 589-6546   *f:* (504) 589-2337

MAINE
Portland, Maine - Jeffrey Porter, Manager
c/o Maine International Trade Center
511 Congress Street, ZIP: 04101
t: (207) 541-7400   *f:* (207) 541-7420

MARYLAND - BALITMORE
Michael Keaveny, Director
World Trade Center, Suite 2432
401 East Pratt Street, ZIP: 21202
t: (410) 962-4539   *f:* (410) 962-4529

A3

MASSACHUSETTS - BOSTON
Frank J. O'Connor, Director
164 Northern Avenue
World Trade Center, Suite 307, ZIP: 02210
t: (617) 424-5990   *f:* (617) 424-5992

MICHIGAN - DETROIT
Neil Hesse, Director
211 W. Fort Street, Suite 2220, ZIP: 48226
t: (313) 226-3650   *f:* (313) 226-3657

MINNESOTA - MINNEAPOLIS
Ronald E. Kramer, Director
45 South 7th St., Suite 2240, ZIP: 55402
t: (612) 348-1638   *f:* (612) 348-1650

MISSISSIPPI
Mississippi - Harrison Ford, Manager
704 East Main St., Raymond, MS, ZIP: 39154
t: (601) 857-0128   *f:* (601) 857-0026

MISSOURI - ST LOUIS
Randall J. LaBounty, Director
8182 Maryland Avenue, Suite 303, ZIP: 63105
t: (314) 425-3302   *f:* (314) 425-3381

MONTANA
Missoula, Montana - Mark Peters, Manager
c/o Montana World Trade Center
Gallagher Business Bldg., Suite 257, ZIP: 59812
t: (406) 243-2098   *f:* (406) 243-5259

NEBRASKA
Omaha, Nebraska - Meredith Bond, Manager
11135 "O" Street, ZIP: 68137
t: (402) 221-3664   *f:* (402) 221-3668

A3

NEVADA
Reno, Nevada - Jere Dabbs, Manager
1755 East Plumb Lane, Suite 152, ZIP: 89502
t: (702) 784-5203   *f:* (702) 784-5343

NEW HAMPSHIRE
Portsmouth, New Hampshire - Susan Berry, Manager
17 New Hampshire Avenue, ZIP: 03801-2838
t: (603) 334-6074   *f:* (603) 334-6110

NEW JERSEY
Trenton, New Jersey - Rod Stuart, Director
3131 Princeton Pike, Bldg. #4, Suite 105, ZIP: 08648
t: (609) 989-2100   *f:* (609) 989-2395

NEW MEXICO
New Mexico - Sandra Necessary, Manager
c/o New Mexico Dept. of Economic Development
P.O. Box 20003, Santa Fe, ZIP: 87504-5003
FEDEX:1100 St. Francis Drive, ZIP: 87503
t: (505) 827-0350   *f:* (505) 827-0263

NEW YORK - NEW YORK
John Lavelle, Acting Director
6 World Trade Center, Rm. 635, ZIP: 10048
t: (212) 466-5222   *f:* (212) 264-1356

NORTH CAROLINA - CAROLINAS
Roger Fortner, Director
521 East Morehead Street, Suite 435, Charlotte, ZIP:
28202
t: (704) 333-4886   *f:* (704) 332-2681

NORTH DAKOTA
Served by the Minneapolis, Minnesota Export
AssistanceCenter

OHIIO - CLEVELAND
Michael Miller, Director
600 Superior Avenue, East, Suite 700
ZIP: 44114
t: (216) 522-4750   *f:* (216) 522-2235

OKLAHOMA
Oklahoma City, Oklahoma - Ronald L. Wilson, Director
301 Northwest 63rd Street, Suite 330, ZIP: 73116
t: (405) 608-5302   *f:* (405) 608-4211

OREGON - PORTLAND
Scott Goddin, Director
One World Trade Center, Suite 242
121 SW Salmon Street, ZIP: 97204
t: (503) 326-3001   *f:* (503) 326-6351

PENNSYLVANIA - PHILADELPHIA
Rod Stuart, Acting Director
615 Chestnut Street, Ste. 1501, ZIP: 19106
t: (215) 597-6101   *f:* (215) 597-6123

PUERTO RICO
San Juan, Puerto Rico (Hato Rey) - Vacant, Manager
525 F.D. Roosevelt Avenue, Suite 905
ZIP: 00918
t: (787) 766-5555   *f:* (787) 766-5692

RHODE ISLAND
Providence, Rhode Island - Vacant, Manager
One West Exchange Street, ZIP: 02903
t: (401) 528-5104, *f:* (401) 528-5067

SOUTH CAROLINA
Columbia, South Carolina - Ann Watts, Director
1835 Assembly Street, Suite 172, ZIP: 29201
t: (803) 765-5345   *f:* (803) 253-3614

A3

SOUTH DAKOTA
Siouxland, South Dakota - Cinnamon King, Manager
Augustana College, 2001 S. Summit Avenue
Room SS-44, Sioux Falls, ZIP: 57197
t: (605) 330-4264   *f:* (605) 330-4266

TENNESSEE
Memphis, Tennessee - Ree Russell, Manager
Buckman Hall, 650 East Parkway South, Suite 348
ZIP: 38104.
t: (901) 323-1543   *f:* (901) 320-9128

TEXAS - DALLAS
LoRee Silloway, Director
P.O. Box 420069, ZIP: 75342-0069
2050 N. Stemmons Fwy., Suite 170, ZIP: 75207
t: (214) 767-0542   *f:* (214) 767-8240

UTAH
Salt Lake City, Utah - Stanley Rees, Director
324 S. State Street, Suite 221, ZIP: 84111
t: (801) 524-5116   *f:* (801) 524-5886

VERMONT
Montpelier, Vermont - Susan Murray, Manager
National Life Building, Drawer 20, ZIP: 05620-0501
t: (802) 828-4508   *f:* (802) 828-3258

VIRGINIA
Richmond, Virginia - Helen D. Lee Hwang, Manager
400 North 8th Street, Suite 540, ZIP: 23240-0026
P.O. Box 10026
t: (804) 771-2246   *f:* (804) 771-2390

WASHINGTON - SEATTLE
David Spann, Director
2001 6th Ave, Suite 650, ZIP: 98121
t: (206) 553-5615   *f:* (206) 553-7253

A3

WEST VIRGINIA
Charleston, West Virginia - Harvey Timberlake, Director
405 Capitol Street, Suite 807, ZIP: 25301
t: (304) 347-5123   *f:* (304) 347-5408

WISCONSIN
Milwaukee, Wisconsin - Paul D. Churchill, Director
517 E. Wisconsin Avenue, Room 596, ZIP: 53202
t: (414) 297-3473   *f:* (414) 297-3470

WYOMING
Served by the Denver, Colorado U.S. Export Assistance
Center.

A3

Gorilla Guides

128 Kensington Church Street, London W8 4BH
Tel: (44) 207 221 7166; Fax: (44) 207 792 9288
E-mail: enquiries@stacey-international.co.uk

business travellers'
H A N D B O O K S

The series that focuses on the needs of the business traveller

The Series

- **Unique:** Nothing like this currently available in the trade market
- **Recognised:** Already widely accepted as the reference by some chambers of commerce and export desks of The Department of Trade and Industry
- **Authoritative:** Highly experienced authors with extensive business experience in the target market

The Business Travellers' Guides to

- Turkey
- Egypt
- Argentina
- The United Arab Emirates
- Saudi Arabia

Content

- **Quality and Efficiency:** Essential tips on where to stay and how to get started
- **Etiquette:** The social morés of the local business culture
- **Creating an Impression:** Where to lunch and dine a local guest; basic vocabulary and phrases
- **The nitty-gritty:** Full details of organisations offering support and advice
- **Business Overviews:** Authoritative insights into the major economic and commercial sectors
- **Contacts:** Appendixes of useful contact details